CHRIS COLSTON
Yours is here

ALL THE KING'S HORSES
~AN EXPRESSION OF DEPRESSION VOLUME 3

Edited by
Nina Antonia
Designed by Chris Colston

LE

LITTLE EPISODES PUBLISHING

ALL THE KING'S HORSES
~ AN EXPRESSION OF DEPRESSION VOLUME 3

The right of the authors in this book to be identified as the authors of their work has been asserted in accordance with the Copyright, Designs and Patents Act 1988

N Antonia is hereby identified as editor of this work in accordance with Sections 77 and 78 of the Copyright, Designs and Patents Act 1988

Any dialogue or behaviour ascribed to the characters in these stories – those who are real people as well as the characters who are imagined – is entirely fictitious. Any resemblance to actual persons, living or dead, is purely coincidental.

All rights reserved. No part of this publication may be reproduced, stored in a retrieval system, or transmitted in any form or by any means, electronic, mechanical, photocopying, recording or otherwise, without prior permission of the copyright owner.

Little Episodes Ltd, No. 7005436

www.LittleEpisodes.org

Design by Chris Colston, London, UK
Printed and bound in Great Britain by Clays Ltd, St Ives Plc.

ISBN 978-0-9565003-3-5

Little Episodes Publishing
Copyright @ Little Episodes Publishing, 2011
First published in Great Britain in 2011 by Little Episodes Publishing.

Edited by Nina Antonia.
With thanks to Nick Ross and Antonia Hodgson at Little, Brown Book Group, Michaela Turner and to all the contributors.

Editor's Preface

2010 was a vicious year. I got whipped by the tail of the Hydra; bereavement, mayhem, hardship. Barely able to stand upright in the maelstrom, a well-meaning soul with mental health training told me that not everyone suffered from depression. I found this very odd. Anyone in their right mind would surely find the world a twisted, difficult place, rife with sorrow. Happiness has always been a fleeting concept, but not for some it would it seem. Those that never doubt their sanity, the rock solids and regular folks, are by and large, dull. Creativity is not wrought from reasonable outlook. It has always been for me something of a blood-letting ritual, a shedding of skin and an escape. In a state of near desperation, I submitted one poem and a prose piece to Little Episodes. Yes, I'd had a career in music journalism and gained more than a little notoriety for chronicling the misadventures of rock n roll drug fiends, but this time it was different. Not a guitar in sight, even if the riffs were still there. I sent the work out into the ether as one might throw a paper plane from a window, expecting no return. And yet, it came several months later with an acceptance note. One overcast Portobello evening, I met with Little Episodes' founding light, Lucie Barat. Over a glass of wine, teeth chattering as we smoked outside The Duke of Wellington, she gave me the keys to the kingdom, the directions to a vision that had been borne out of experience.

I hate the word 'Community' it smacks of alfalfa and Birkenstock. I much prefer 'Resistance Movement,' for this is what Little Episodes represents, an artistic platform that raises awareness of addiction and mental health with none of the 'I'm well, you're ill' imbalance of traditional systems. Anyone who doesn't recognise the maladies within themselves is less of a human being for it. I am immeasurably grateful to Lucie and Little Episodes' designer, Chris Colston, for giving me the opportunity to be 'Editor In Chief' of 'All the King's Horses' and to Jerome Alexandre for his encouragement. The quality of submissions was extremely high and the pleasure of sorting the rubies from the dust, all mine.

NINA ANTONIA—FEBRUARY, 2011

ACCOLADES FOR LITTLEEPISODES.ORG

LE, a buzzing hub indeed. I have written on a few other sites, and most of them you wade through blatant bashing and teen angst before you got any good material or good feedback (praise or honest criticism). I would take this moment to thank everyone here for contributing material, so my broke ass doesn't have to go buy books to find good reading material...and we're saving trees in the process.

~ DAVID PAUL GESSNER (LE MEMBER)

Thank you for the kind words on Paradise Cove. I am honored to be part of such an important movement. LE inspires me to write daily, free to continue to explore the artistic journey, breaking all boundaries. Thank you for the raw source of talent and energy you bring together as a collective group.

~ JACQEULINE CIOFFA (LE MEMBER)

It is indeed an honour to be associated with this site – worthy in so many ways, with talented people.

~ DIANE NELSON (LE MEMBER)

This is like a head clean Bohemian dream. I know I've found more inspiration here than I ever did at the bottom of a bag or bottle. I may be the least of the brilliant talent pool here, but I am number 1 when it comes to appreciation of what's offered here! All the best to all of you!

~ROLF OCALE (LE MEMBER)

Expression of Depression Anthology Series
Mission Statement

I would consider myself to have been lost. Perhaps I provoked myself with persistent existential angst, or perhaps I just struggled with life and finding my place in the world.

I have spent time on psychologists' couches and I have resided in various institutions, and in the end, I believe I became 'found.' On my journey, I read empathetic accounts of other people's experiences. It helped to lift the 'bell jar' a little when I felt imprisoned in the battleground of my mind and when I felt most alone on the edges of society.

I wanted to create something that might provide light and understanding to other sufferers of depression, mental illness, or just people struggling. I also wanted to provide a platform for talented artists who have never had a 'break,' as it's well known that most artistic industries can be harsh on even the most happy of personalities. Plenty of talented people fall by the wayside simply because they don't have the fight or the thick skin to keep playing the artistic lottery for a chance at success. Both Little Episodes Publishing and Little Episodes Productions feature work from successful, as well as unknown, talent.

Most of all, I wanted to help de-stigmatise depression and promote compassion and understanding rather than fear and embarrassment. I also wanted to dispel the notion that depression is in any way cool. I wanted to express the belief that romantic dead poets and the image of sultry, tragic heroines are just a dangerous mirage. If you flirt with a glamorised dark side, you could fall through, and contrary to popular belief, you will not discover a font of creative inspiration, but quite the opposite: a dull, flat hell land.

LUCIE BARÂT 2009

CONTENTS

Editor's Preface		*i*
Accolades for LittleEpisodes.org		*iii*
Expression of Depression Anthology Series		
Mission Statement		*iv*
LUCIE BARÂT	*The Bang Beat*	1
EVA DESTRUCTION	*Junkferatu*	2
HELEN R. PETERSON	*Jesus Loves Me in Mandarin*	4
IAIN PETTITT	*Oft the Road Most Travelled*	5
BERI ANN MILLER	*7*	9
JAMES CAGNEY	*I Learned Crazy from my Cousin John Edward*	10
SARAH MACMANUS	*Balcony Scene*	12
ANN TINKHAM	*Frozen Lace*	13
CAROLINE RYDER	*The Audition*	16
MICHAELA TURNER	*The Absence of Life*	24
NINA ANTONIA	*Invocation of My Demon Sister*	26
MICHAEL BUTLER	*Reflections*	28
SADIE FROST	*Dad's Nose*	34
LUCIE BARÂT	*Locked in*	35
COLIN MCKAY MILLER	*The Next Thing to Go*	36
BERI ANN MILLER	*12*	40
DANNY MCCOSH	*New Year's Eve*	41
FEDERICA FREZZA	*The Fool*	42
DAVE VEGAS	*My Confession*	45
FRAN LOCK	*Virgil Navigates Hell*	47
JEROME ALEXANDRE	*Drought Season*	50
NINA ANTONIA	*Sorry*	54
NADIA KHOMAMI	*All Hallows Eve*	55
CIARA BURKE	*Libertine*	58
COLLEEN ALLEN	*RIP*	60
ANNA KIRK	*Wholesome*	63

EILIDH MACDONALD	*Self Portrait at the Lowry*	64
ISAAC JAMES BAKER	*This is Gregory Sampson*	65
DOMINIC STEVENSON	*The Person Opposite on the Train*	74
JACK VARNELL / THE EMOTIONAL ORPHAN	*Flashes*	75
NINA ANTONIA	*The End of the World Is Nice*	76
JACK COOPER	*Upstairs*	78
LUCIE BARÂT	*Me, twice*	79
KJERSTI FURU	*I Got A Balinese Dancing Girl Tattooed Across My Chest*	82
DANNY McCOSH	*Bowing Out in Bow*	83
FRAN LOCK	*Feme Sole*	84
RHIANNON WILLIAMS	*A Letter to My Little Brother*	86
MICHAELA TURNER	*A Riddle*	89
EMMA JONES	*Tell Me About Your Father*	90

Little Episodes Mission Statement

British intelligentsia welcomed him with open arms because 'dirty' Lenny was hipper than hip. Hip was originally opium den terminology, a reference to the sore spot one got from hours spent in sideways repose, chasing clouds. And who didn't have a copy of Burroughs' *Junky* and the Stones' *Beggars Banquet*? Twin pillars of stone cold cool. It wasn't until the 1980s, when cheap heroin became widely available to any old Janet and John that politicians started to get fussed. Opium for the people just wasn't on. Even then there was a modicum of sympathy. That is until the tabloids headed up the witchhunt and fanned the flames. I smell the kindling in town squares and job centres. Billie Holiday's gardenias, the golden scent of Xanadu, gone forever.

HELEN R. PETERSON
Jesus Loves Me in Mandarin

Listening to the Chinese church sing "Great
Is Thy Faithfulness" in the lower room
while trying to keep my mind on Bible
study and the baby off the table, feels
like Jesus is tired of my West Hem. posturing,
my whine, my cheese, my pretty please
says don't tell Me about pain, try a spear
in the side, girl, your sister texts
you in the middle of the night,
My brothers called me crazy
you sitting around singing empty bed blues?
My friends couldn't even sit up one night
For Me, denied Me, and here I was, cat o' 9
up the behind, thorns crammed in My skull
for their sorry asses, and yours—

IAIN PETTITT
Oft the Road Most Travelled

'Oft the road most travelled, will be yours,' my mother used to say to me. She was an ambiguous figure, and so every Friday, I would sit in my armchair and muse upon her philosophies. Alas, it was Thursday, and I must go to her grave for afternoon tea and the ritualistic bringing of flowers. Bucky drove me there, like he did every Thursday afternoon, and he was almost as ambiguous as my mother, except he was a man, so his ambiguousness was less of a mystery to me and to everyone he ever spoke to. A large chap, but thin as a rake, and as enthusiastic as one too. I always stare at the grey hairs on the bottom of his neck that slowly run their way, streaking through the furrows of a gorgeous mane. I have never seen his face, and I wouldn't like to, either, because you can always tell a man's face from his voice, and he spoke gravelly words that sputtered into my ears, and gave the whole trip to my mother's grave a certain—

I called him Bucky because he reminded me of an old Alsatian I used to have; he was grey from birth and always walked with a limp. Bucky had a limp, but only in my head.

'I say, Bucky, could we drive a little slower today, please? I feel a little queasy in the sunshine, Bucky.'

'As always, sir.'

The drive took much longer than I intended, but I suppose seeing all the weeping willows between my house and the graveyard is a splendour. Sometimes it's just nice to put your hands out and brush against the trees; it's almost ethereal.

'Do you like Willows, Bucky? I find they have a morbid feeling, Bucky. What's your favourite tree, Bucky'?

'Trees are good, sir.'

'Yes I know, Bucky, but what's your favourite? You have to have an opinion, Bucky, life demands it.'

'Lemon trees, sir.'

'No good, Bucky, not for your nature. You need a mellower tree. How about the oak, Bucky?'

'Very good, sir.'

The gates to the graveyard are my favourite gates in the world; they are rusty, but you can see the splendid jet-black paint that used to adorn it, scattered on the ground in little flakes. There were less flakes than the last time I came, but jet-black flakes can be rather tasty.

Mother's grave was a statue, but it didn't depict her. It was a statue of Zeus, sitting on his throne on Mount Olympus. Mother always used to say, 'A grave is your life, make it splendid.' So, when she finally kicked the bucket, I had it made for her. I know mother would be proud. You can see why Zeus was the chief God in Greek times; his genitals were massive, protruding from his body like a fist, ready to thrash Hera to oblivion.

'Oh Mother, why did you leave me? Was I a bad boy? Did I not feed you enough tuna sandwiches?'

She never answered back, but I knew it was because of the sandwiches. She loved to snack on them, sometimes fifty rounds of sandwiches a day, and she got bigger and bigger, until one day she stopped eating sandwiches altogether. I think it was then that she died, for she got thinner and thinner until she withered to nothingness and slipped into her grave.

Bucky gave a loud honk on the horn, loud enough to interrupt my thoughts, but quiet enough to keep mother calm.

'Yes, Bucky! Coming, Bucky!' I howled at the top of my voice, shaking the flakes a little with my tremendous, booming voice

I sat in the seat at the back of the car, leant down and picked up a few flakes from the floor and put them in my pocket for later.

'Drive me home, Bucky.'

'Very good, sir.'

There are no willows on the way home, just a bland, brown wall that I can barely trace my fingers along, the soggy moss sticking to the tips of my fingers and remaining there until my afternoon tea break.

'I say, Bucky, could we drive a little slower today, please? I feel a little queasy in the sunshine, Bucky.'

'As always, sir.'

7

As I turn away
my scuffs align
creating a caped giant
leaning over me
my cut finger follows the
path formed by cracks
leading to a heart
belonging to a man with a key
though the whispers from
the cobble stones
imply there's no finding it
my breath has nowhere else to waste
its time
other than in the back of my throat
waiting
My dress of wire twigs and nails
rubs at the exposed muscle of my thigh
my body is too exhausted to
bleed
children skipping along my skin
yawns of trees clinging to my skull
scars up my back forming a
zipper
how you unzip so secretly
sends chills through
my force field
strapping mirrors to my split feet
with my eyes closed
I can still feel the ache
in my spirit
my hair laced with

LUCIE BARÂT
The Bang Beat

It's the dirty end of the day, the interval between the
fiery footed steeds
and the cloak that makes immoral acts more wholesome.
Lazy light and seedy exchanges
go together penis in hand, so to speak.
An extra rent boost before the night shift—
when I work harder than
a cat covering crap on a marble floor, as it were.

I'm perched against an open door on Peter Street, thinking that
if I can catch myself a suited trick from the Soho flow
short-cutting from commuter street, I can catch
myself a treat from G Man while his batch is fresh.
When he first stands out on his piss-marked patch, like a
crack riddled Pied Piper knowing his Toms will come,
like a nose following Bisto...

But there's junk among the trade during this arse end of the day,
and no one ever seems to mind yesterday's puke
splattering the concrete. Faceless, casually clad tourists
wonder through in their oblivious
bell jars.
They smile and stop to commit me to a Kodak moment,
like I'm a mirage, like they're considering an art installation,
like they're enjoying a piece of street theatre, like there
won't be blood and cum and a down-and-out cheek on that spot
later on, where they stand with leisure-footed feet,
and I have to say,
I feel violated and abused. I feel sold short and used
while I'm just waiting, minding my own business
looking for an extra-curricular trick to fund me a little treat.

EVA DESTRUCTION
Junkferatu

In the tabloid imagination, there is no creature lower than Junkferatu. It will come for your children, taint the neighbourhood, and destroy communities. Recently, a government minister, tie as tight as a noose, announced that under alliance rule, Britain will soon be a drug-free nation. The bogey-man stalks the shadows of Whitehall, not the streets of the UK. It is the junkie's own body that is his foe, with its eternal cycle of need, rather than a society that judges him a penny-dreadful caricature. Nonetheless, plans are afoot to sanction the benefits of anyone who admits or is suspected of getting high. People who may never before have thought about stealing may be left with little choice. Alternative prescribing is to be phased out, robbing thousands of fragile stability. Across Europe, Latin America and the US, moderation and even decriminalisation are being considered, but in Blighty, we tighten the screws. Before his rise, David Cameron appealed to the UN to legalise drugs, now he panders to tabloid-generated moral panic. Theresa May launched the latest drugs strategy in December 2010, peppered with feisty rhetoric of the 'Hunt 'em down, smoke 'em out, place garlic at your windows' variety. Round up the hags, whores, skid-row scumbags, shiv-wielding somnambulists who constitute Junkferatu's ragged legion. It never used to be this way.

Just how did the junkie stereotype evolve into a figure of contempt? At the root is class. Yesteryear's vamps and fops, Crowley, De Quincey, Coleridge, Baudelaire, the fab four of opium reveries, were educated and of means. Well-bred aesthetes were pardoned for their trespass on the grounds of creativity and breeding. The first casualties hailed from the Jazz realm, real gone cats, Charlie Parker, Chet Baker, yet still the élan of style and mystique lingered, for these were blue note Gods, at least for awhile. Lenny Bruce was the warning shot, although

British intelligentsia welcomed him with open arms because 'dirty' Lenny was hipper than hip. Hip was originally opium den terminology, a reference to the sore spot one got from hours spent in sideways repose, chasing clouds. And who didn't have a copy of Burroughs' *Junky* and the Stones' *Beggars Banquet*? Twin pillars of stone cold cool. It wasn't until the 1980s, when cheap heroin became widely available to any old Janet and John that politicians started to get fussed. Opium for the people just wasn't on. Even then there was a modicum of sympathy. That is until the tabloids headed up the witchhunt and fanned the flames. I smell the kindling in town squares and job centres. Billie Holiday's gardenias, the golden scent of Xanadu, gone forever.

HELEN R. PETERSON
Jesus Loves Me in Mandarin

Listening to the Chinese church sing "Great
Is Thy Faithfulness" in the lower room
while trying to keep my mind on Bible
study and the baby off the table, feels
like Jesus is tired of my West Hem. posturing,
my whine, my cheese, my pretty please
says don't tell Me about pain, try a spear
in the side, girl, your sister texts
you in the middle of the night,
My brothers called me crazy
you sitting around singing empty bed blues?
My friends couldn't even sit up one night
For Me, denied Me, and here I was, cat o' 9
up the behind, thorns crammed in My skull
for their sorry asses, and yours—

IAIN PETTITT
Oft the Road Most Travelled

'Oft the road most travelled, will be yours,' my mother used to say to me. She was an ambiguous figure, and so every Friday, I would sit in my armchair and muse upon her philosophies. Alas, it was Thursday, and I must go to her grave for afternoon tea and the ritualistic bringing of flowers. Bucky drove me there, like he did every Thursday afternoon, and he was almost as ambiguous as my mother, except he was a man, so his ambiguousness was less of a mystery to me and to everyone he ever spoke to. A large chap, but thin as a rake, and as enthusiastic as one too. I always stare at the grey hairs on the bottom of his neck that slowly run their way, streaking through the furrows of a gorgeous mane. I have never seen his face, and I wouldn't like to, either, because you can always tell a man's face from his voice, and he spoke gravelly words that sputtered into my ears, and gave the whole trip to my mother's grave a certain—

I called him Bucky because he reminded me of an old Alsatian I used to have; he was grey from birth and always walked with a limp. Bucky had a limp, but only in my head.

'I say, Bucky, could we drive a little slower today, please? I feel a little queasy in the sunshine, Bucky.'

'As always, sir.'

The drive took much longer than I intended, but I suppose seeing all the weeping willows between my house and the graveyard is a splendour. Sometimes it's just nice to put your hands out and brush against the trees; it's almost ethereal.

'Do you like Willows, Bucky? I find they have a morbid feeling, Bucky. What's your favourite tree, Bucky'?

'Trees are good, sir.'

'Yes I know, Bucky, but what's your favourite? You have to have an opinion, Bucky, life demands it.'

'Lemon trees, sir.'

'No good, Bucky, not for your nature. You need a mellower tree. How about the oak, Bucky?'

'Very good, sir.'

The gates to the graveyard are my favourite gates in the world; they are rusty, but you can see the splendid jet-black paint that used to adorn it, scattered on the ground in little flakes. There were less flakes than the last time I came, but jet-black flakes can be rather tasty.

Mother's grave was a statue, but it didn't depict her. It was a statue of Zeus, sitting on his throne on Mount Olympus. Mother always used to say, 'A grave is your life, make it splendid.' So, when she finally kicked the bucket, I had it made for her. I know mother would be proud. You can see why Zeus was the chief God in Greek times; his genitals were massive, protruding from his body like a fist, ready to thrash Hera to oblivion.

'Oh Mother, why did you leave me? Was I a bad boy? Did I not feed you enough tuna sandwiches?'

She never answered back, but I knew it was because of the sandwiches. She loved to snack on them, sometimes fifty rounds of sandwiches a day, and she got bigger and bigger, until one day she stopped eating sandwiches altogether. I think it was then that she died, for she got thinner and thinner until she withered to nothingness and slipped into her grave.

Bucky gave a loud honk on the horn, loud enough to interrupt my thoughts, but quiet enough to keep mother calm.

'Yes, Bucky! Coming, Bucky!' I howled at the top of my voice, shaking the flakes a little with my tremendous, booming voice

I sat in the seat at the back of the car, leant down and picked up a few flakes from the floor and put them in my pocket for later.

'Drive me home, Bucky.'

'Very good, sir.'

There are no willows on the way home, just a bland, brown wall that I can barely trace my fingers along, the soggy moss sticking to the tips of my fingers and remaining there until my afternoon tea break.

'I say, Bucky, could we drive a little slower today, please? I feel a little queasy in the sunshine, Bucky.'

'As always, sir.'

BERI ANN MILLER

7

As I turn away
my scuffs align
creating a caped giant
leaning over me
my cut finger follows the
path formed by cracks
leading to a heart
belonging to a man with a key
though the whispers from
the cobble stones
imply there's no finding it
my breath has nowhere else to waste
its time
other than in the back of my throat
waiting
My dress of wire twigs and nails
rubs at the exposed muscle of my thigh
my body is too exhausted to
bleed
children skipping along my skin
yawns of trees clinging to my skull
scars up my back forming a
zipper
how you unzip so secretly
sends chills through
my force field
strapping mirrors to my split feet
with my eyes closed
I can still feel the ache
in my spirit
my hair laced with

illness
pain
and poison
Teeth ground down
by
too many tastes
of black silky
sleepy permanence.

JAMES CAGNEY
*** I Learned Crazy from my Cousin John Edward ***

take your aunt for a substitute momma
she'll help you get new apartments every year

be your only visitor in art deco hospitals
that serve hypodermic lunches

know the police by name. know god by name.
know the devil by name—but get them confused

sleep in the park when the walls
start closing in. be polite to birds

sprinkle lithium on your breakfast cereal
draw perfect freehand apostles and arch

angels drifting down like puppets from orange
and yellow heavens. misquote parts of revelation

that best articulate your case
sit at bus stops and stare wide eyed

at the hot bowl of the sun. burst
apartment walls open with your heart

keep secrets that would blow up the earth
but let no one forget you have that power

talk shit to demons and pick your afro
with the rib cages of angels

get drunk and become angry moses
use furniture for tablets. warn the voices

partying within the nature of god's wrath
use malt liquor for holy water

crucify yourself know everyone
awaiting your second coming is dead

SARAH MACMANUS
Balcony Scene

Little brother,
that spark behind your eyes
that beats on the walls
and screams bloody murder;
it got caught in my throat, see?
Hammers against my chest
and rattles my bones

Take my hand,
we'll scream together.

Little brother,
that catch in your voice
that swallows the pain
and smashes the glasses;
I got drunk on that, see?
It spins my head
and pounds in my ears

Take my hand,
we'll smash them all.

ANN TINKHAM
Frozen Lace

As I sit on the bathroom floor, a deflated parasail, all I can hear is the *drip, drip, drip* of the almost overflowing claw-foot bathtub. I picked this place because of its Victorian-era charm, and now I realise it was a genius move because the bathtub is so deep. The new-fangled hotels have shallow tubs. That just wouldn't do.

I should mention that the drip, drip, dripping is interrupted by Sidney's snoring. Forget sawing logs; he sounds like a chainsaw.

I'm wondering how to arrange myself—wedding gown and all—into this 1920s-era tub. When I shopped for my gown with the mother of the bride (aka my mom) and we both fell in love with the train, who knew that the train would trip me up in my final hours.

I'm not sure what happens once I submerge myself and the gown. It will be like holding my breath under water, but when I start to gasp, I'll stay down there. Then I'll start taking in water like an ill-fated ship at sea. Finally it will be ship ahoy, mate overboard, sunken mermaid, and slimy seaweed hair. At what point will I know the job's done? I guess that's the point. I won't know.

Bride Drowns in Gown. At first they'll suspect foul play. Then Sidney will have his alibi—drunken stupor—on his wedding night. No need for a note; the world will know why.

I'm in and under but every time I start to breathe in water, I choke, cough and surface. The human body is hardwired against this stuff. I'll try again. I'll imagine the water is air and inhale deeply—deep sea kundalini. This time, water is going into and out of my nose and making me cry.

And I can't stop crying. Tears are welling up and trickling down my cheeks, my mouth, my chin, now pouring into the bathwater. I can taste the saltiness of my tears.

Then a strange thing happens.

The salt makes me want to live. Not because I'm a big fan of saline. The tang of salt on my tongue makes me hurt for myself.

I grab onto the red porcelain sides of the tub and push myself up; the water level drops dramatically. I catch my image in the mirror. I look like the drowned Bride of Frankenstein with blackened rivulets of mascara cascading down my cheeks, my French roll drenched, bloodshot eyes under blue eye shadow and a mid-scream horror movie mouth that scares even me.

I don't recommend bathing in a wedding dress, in case you were considering it. As soon as I feel the drenched satin and lace against my skin, I'm sniffing and shivering. Even so, I slip into my ivory bridal pumps and scurry/tiptoe past the human chainsaw, who would have slept through my drowning incident and woken up to coffee and a bloated bride. That would teach him to not drink and wed. Save the lesson for another wedding day, another bride.

I'm out the hotel room door in a soggy flash, my dress dripping and the train leaving a damp trail on the carpet. Lucky for me it's lights out at the bed and breakfast; otherwise, soggy bride leaving hotel alone after midnight might send the wrong message.

The other thing I don't recommend is getting married in New England in December, just in case you decide against drowning yourself after submerging in your gown, and then flee the scene.

Once I'm outside in the single digit temps, it takes all of a minute for the satin and lace to freeze into a leaden, gown-shaped snowflake with me as a human dress stand. But if there is pain due to impending frostbite, I don't notice. My eyes, which moments ago would have become water-logged orbs, are turned upward toward the spiralling snowflakes, coating the bed and breakfast's lamp post and rod iron fence. My fingers, which would have become clammy, blue digits are being tickled with flakes and melting them into moisture droplets. My feet, nearly swollen and limp, are carrying me across the crunching, crystalline snow to the highway.

As I approach, a 1950s Cadillac pulls over. I do a double-take. Is it actually pink? A man's face appears as his window opens. If I didn't know better, I'd have guessed he was the ghost of Elvis.

'You all right, miss?'
'Where are you headed?'
'Memphis.'
'Me, too!'
'In a frozen wedding gown?'
'And you in a pink Cadillac?'

CAROLINE RYDER
The Audition

It was 113 degrees in downtown Los Angeles, and hotel parking attendants stuffed cans of ice-cold Coke Zero in their jackets and pants, cursing the uncompromising *calor*. A few miles northwest, in the shimmering hills above Hollywood, Desmond Furie masturbated alone by his infinity pool. In his head, he relived the best scenes from the heat of his own adolescence, weaving them with the most outré storylines from his films, a slimmer version of himself in the starring role. It was the most oppressive day in the city's meteorological history, and the air smelled like black sage and dust. It was also his birthday.

Desmond dumped the dregs of his rooibus tea into the pool and pulled himself off the sun lounger, his skin coated in sunscreen and lube. The view from his 1938 estate was magnificent, and in the distance, the smog hung low over downtown, a thick layer of green mist layered with orange and dirty white, melting into a rapidly dimming sky. Inside the house, Desmond ignored the empty tubs of medical marijuana that were scattered on the granite kitchen counter—the housekeeper would deal with those later. He took off his silver locket. Once upon a time it would have been filled with cocaine in wry homage to Weimar era slut Anita Berber, whom his girlfriend more than resembled. Today it held a blend of pure, high-grade valerian root powder, 'nature's downer,' his healer had told him.

Desmond Furie was an independent film director who had established himself with one teen exploitation movie in 1987, a masterpiece of experimental storytelling called *A Minor*. He had spent every year since *A Minor* watching himself become further removed from the youthful subject matter that had made his name. Today, the first day of his sixth decade, he ached to escape his paunchy decrepitude. His girlfriend, a 24-year-old actress/writer called Tiara Loomis who had famously performed on-screen fellatio in one of his art films—'groundbreaking smut' according to *Variety*—knew better than to be around Desmond on his birthday. (She was in Milan, meeting with a fashion designer about directing her next advertising campaign.)

Desmond snorted a bump of valerian powder, showered, and got dressed. Wearing a black T-shirt, black Levis, black sneakers and prescription self-correcting sunglasses, he got into his black BMW and set the air conditioning to max. 'Get out of the way, fucker,' he snarled at the sedan blocking the right turn lane ahead of him. His iPod played gangsta rap and Japanese heavy metal on shuffle. He drove fast. It took him about 20 minutes to get to the intersection of Washington and Crenshaw, where Caviar lived.

Caviar was a rapper. A British music writer had sent Desmond some of Caviar's videos with a note saying 'this shit is swag.' Desmond watched, entranced. This shit *was* swag, the most swag shit he had seen in a long time. Caviar rapped about rape, about scat, about swastikas, and about ass-fucking little teenage black girls in graveyards. 'Youthful innocence,' Desmond had once told a room full of investors, 'is interesting only by virtue of its absence.' As such, Caviar was perfect for his next movie. New, angry, fucked-up and delicious, Caviar's defiantly languid lower lip and invasively dark lyrical bent made Desmond feel the same way he felt when he was shooting potato guns in the desert at age seven, getting high off the tubular *thunk* the potatoes made as they traveled high into the universe. Caviar reminded him what it felt like when he shot speed into his arm at age 17, and, aged 47, scored street heroin with the hugely talented young star of his latest movie. Not long after, in that same alleyway, he was busted by undercover, and this time his agent, TC Dreddsnik, wasn't able to keep it quiet. 'One more arrest,' TC said, 'and you're finished.' And that's when Desmond Furie, already well into his mid-fifties and legendary for his Herculean resistance to sobriety, finally decided to get clean.

He worked the Steps alongside all the other A-list, out-of-work substance fiends in town, admitting he was powerless over alcohol, acknowledging that his life had become unmanageable, and realizing that he was, on most days, the oldest motherfucker in the room. There was a summer, a few years into Desmond's new sober life, when the fires burned the green slopes around his home, charring the natural chaparral gardens of Dante's View and Captain's Roost, making them barren and tarred as the 405 freeway. That brush fire, on May 8, 2007, marked the last time he had felt inspired since quitting the drugs—until Caviar. 'I think I have something,' he texted TC.

The kid was elusive—no contact info on his blog—but Desmond managed to track Caviar down by asking his personal publicist, who also represented the Wu Tang Clan, to Tweet at Caviar. Caviar responded. Before long Desmond had the kid's phone number. 'Meet me at my grandmother's hair salon,' Caviar had said on the telephone, his voice deep for a 16-year-old's. Desmond pulled into a strip mall occupied by a liquor store, a bar, and Caviar's grandma's hairdressing salon. It was called 'Addictionz'. Caviar was waiting for him, sitting on the curb outside the salon with a skateboard beneath his feet, rolling it from side to side.

Earlier that day, after leaving his mom's house, Caviar had thrown his skateboard to the ground, propelling himself using his left leg like an oar. Steady, with the *clack clack* of hard wheels on concrete, he had burned through neighborhood after neighborhood, oblivious to the hot pink bougainvillea that seemed to sigh and wilt as he shot by. The whole city was on fire, yet Caviar kept on his Davy Crocket hunter's hat, its floppy ears absorbing the rivulets of sweat that tumbled from his temples.

Desmond watched Caviar pull out a bundle of keys and unlock the door to the salon. 'You must be hot under those fluffy ears,' he said, feeling like a dick the second he said it. Caviar didn't say anything. 'I really dig your rhymes, Caviar.' Inside, ragged leather chairs were haphazardly positioned in front of dusty mirrors, and the lighting was so unforgiving, Desmond wished that he too had worn a hat. Styrofoam heads in full makeup and crowned with cheap wigs sat in a neat line on a shelf, watching as Caviar locked the door behind them. There was no air conditioning and Desmond felt his body heat billow beneath his T-shirt, warming his silver locket as he followed Caviar into a small apartment at the back. It smelled yeasty in there, like old cheeseburgers. A framed portrait of Jesus Christ sat on the mantle.

In the kitchen, Caviar took a blender out of the cupboard. He pulled a bag out of his pocket and waved it in the air. It contained at least an ounce of weed. He poured it into the blender. He opened up his backpack and pulled more plastic baggies from its depths. He began pouring powders, herbs, pills and liquids into the glass jug. At least 30 pills, it looked like. Desmond was first to break the silence.

'One time we were shooting in Vietnam—I mean, shooting a film—and in the regular drug stores they sell everything—like, everything. Morphine, dialudid, oxycontin, whatever. And the beer's cheap as shit. You ever been to Vietnam?'

Caviar shook his head. The cheap bamboo blinds had been drawn all the way down and the kitchen surfaces were grimy. Desmond noticed an eviction notice on the counter and wondered where Caviar's grandmother was and if she was older than he was. 'You and me Caviar, we're the same,' he said. 'We are the hunters and the gatherers. The survivors.'

Caviar pulled out another baggie. It was filled with a yellowy white powder of unknown composition. Next up, a green liquid. Robitussin. Next up, another brand of cough medicine, this time red. Caviar poured the whole bottle into the blender. Desmond already knew that Caviar was going to make him drink whatever evil poisonous shit he was making. It looked like every single possible Class A, B and C substance on earth would be represented in Caviar's smoothie. Desmond had done a lot of drugs in his life—but he'd never done them all at once.

Caviar walked to the fridge, pulled out a beer and opened it with his teeth, spitting the cap onto the floor and taking a swig. Then he poured the remainder of the bottle into the blender. The mixture was alive, foaming, mottled by with the pink and the green of the cough syrups, looking like all the smog that had ever hovered above Los Angeles had been suctioned up and dumped into this jug, resulting in a concoction that might have been thrown up by a homeless person a few weeks ago. The lid went on the appliance and Desmond watched in silence as Caviar hit 'blend.'

Caviar stopped, and poured the mixture into red plastic cups. He handed one to Desmond. The old dude's nerves had already irritated Caviar, and when Desmond recoiled, it irked the boy into verbal expression. 'Shit. They told me you were cool. I could be catering to some bitch right now. Bitches equal money, money equals time, time equals money, money equals bitches. Are you come using my game? Who you think you were?'

Under the heat of Caviar's glare, Desmond recalled the deranged eyes of the armed Congolese border patrolman he had encountered in 1982, back when he was still traveling international brothels and getting high. Desmond's guide had urged him to remove his aviator sunglasses, assuring him it would placate the guard, and it had worked. Tonight, Desmond had no sunglasses to remove. No Plan B. 'You with me now?' Caviar said, his voice rising. 'Cause I only work with family, and *this*, motherfucker, *this* is how we make family, unless yo daughter's gonna be pregnant with my ho.' Caviar snickered.

Desmond thought about family for a second. He had never met his father. His mother was drunk on gin and Tramadol in Palm Springs. His little sister OD'd a long time ago. He had never knowingly sired any children. Tiara was fucking Italian lesbians, and TC wasn't returning his calls. Desmond drank the mixture quickly, trying to stay in control of the nausea that immediately welled up in his stomach and through his esophagus. 'Fuck you, Caviar,' he spluttered, vile chemicals numbing his gums. Caviar's eyes rolled back in his head as he swallowed, slow and hard. *Glug. Gulp. Gulp.* His Adam's apple throbbed. Desmond lunged toward the kitchen sink and threw up.

About 15 minutes later, Desmond became vaguely aware that he and Caviar had left the salon. And he was aware that they were walking into a liquor store. Those were the only hard facts he could establish. Desmond was seeing the world as he would through a fisheye lens, bent and curved, and was still sane enough to know he was experiencing a special kind of delirium, one in which panic would be accompanied by extreme physical torpor. He searched clumsily for his silver locket, his hands like paddles as they tried to open the antique clasp. He poured the contents into his mouth, turning his teeth the color of cinnamon. 'We need all your plant-based sedatives,' he begged the store attendant, a cloud of valerian puffing from his mouth as he clung to the counter for balance.

He felt Caviar's arms around him, dragging him out of the liquor store. 'I'm…currently unused…to chemical extremism,' he slurred, knowing that it would be hard to walk without clinging to the walls. Perhaps they needed more uppers in order to regain balance. 'There's no dignity left,' he wailed as Caviar draped him on to his skateboard, his arms and legs splayed. Caviar started pushing him along the sidewalk, and Desmond's fingernails scraped on the sidewalk. *Clack, clack.*

This is no way to travel, Desmond thought. *Clack, clack.* 'TC will send a car for us—where's my Blackberry.' Desmond was aware of light, dark, approximate shapes, vomit and the blood which was pouring from his nose. Someone was screaming, and he wasn't sure if it was him or Caviar, who was holding his hands to his ears. Desmond's mind drifted to Sarah Palin and gospel music and convention centers filled with elderly, white southerners. 'The Death Star is coming,' he sang. 'Old people in motorized scooters—they're surrounding us! Government is not the solution and government is not the problem. Fuck you! Medicare is socialized medicine! I am on Medicare right now you motherfuckers and *you're going to pay for it!*'

'Um…you guys okay?'

A shadow leaned over Desmond, who was still prostrate on Caviar's skateboard, his arms up in a broad gesture, reaching for God like the Joshua Trees that grew around his boyhood desert home. Caviar was a few yards away peeing in a mailbox.

'We are *not* okay. We need PVC pipe, PVC primer, a drill and some Aquanet, for ignition,' said Desmond, eyes rolling. 'And potatoes, lots of potatoes. We need to defend ourselves.' The shadow backed away, slowly.

Desmond looked up at the stars. 'We don't have Aquanet,' he whispered, remembering what his birthday horoscope said that morning. 'No pressure, Libra, but as things are now, you might want to evaluate your career. Is it working out well?' His hand clutched his Blackberry and Desmond dialed TC over and over, realizing, in sadness, that he could no longer downward scroll, as the darkness slowly but utterly consumed him.

Desmond opened his eyes. He got on his knees. His inner ear was humming and throbbing and his skin pulsed. Caviar lay before him, his skin grey under the light of the moon. Blood poured from his gums and dripped from his nose and his lean stomach muscles no longer rolled and shuddered. One, maybe two molars were on the ground and Caviar's eyes had rolled completely back into his head while foam poured from his mouth like this morning's cappuccino. Desmond rested his head on Caviar's chest. His Blackberry vibrated. Blue and red lights closed in, flashing about them softly, like northern lights in a disco. Desmond took the call. 'I think we found our guy, TC,' he slurred, wondering, as he was led into the backseat of the patrol car, who had called a cab.

MICHAELA TURNER
The Absence of Life

You sat on the day bed
sticking pins in the map
of your veins, picking
destinations ever more remote,
going nowhere again and again.

Your house was
full of dead things;
I didn't know mine
would be too, soon.

A mummified cat
down a hole
in the garden
could be sold at
the antique market,
you agreed.

Bright-feathered birds,
fooled by the false-azure
of your windowpanes,
lay perfectly lifeless
on your bathroom carpet.
When I told you,
you said you knew.

And that wooden box
of miniature mammals
you presented to us
on the kitchen table:
'You'll end up like that shrew,

if you're not careful,'
I said, trying to be funny.

I came home in your
red England shirt,
the sleeves stained
with the darker red
of your blood.

It gave Mother the creeps
and she washed it.
It's lost now—
like most things.

NINA ANTONIA
Invocation of My Demon Sister

Cain's daughter
Thinner
Than
Paper
Poetry
Of
Scant Currency
Build me up
Buttercup
I'm living
On
Never Enough
Moonbeams
In my purse
Twigs for bones
The serenade
Of
Dead men's trombones
Cobweb crescent
Scarecrow smile
Boots worn down
By
Too many miles
Got me a broomstick
So
I can fly
I'd rather be
The bride of Frankenstein
Than working
9-5
Build me up

Buttercup
We'll get by
On
Never Enough
A banquet of books
The scent of the woods
Secrets of iniquity
Lost in antiquity
Our Crowley
Who art in Thelema
Why are there holes
In the pockets
Of
Dreamers?
Why are there holes
In the souls
Of
Dreamers?

MICHAEL BUTLER
Reflections

She'd been reading since she woke at 2 a.m. after a visit to the bathroom and had to hold the book at an angle to get the most out of the crummy bed-side light. She didn't want to wake him.

'Wow.'

He was just drifting back into reality after a deep, dreamless sleep.

'Wow.' She rolled over on to her front, feet becoming tangled in crumpled, cream sheets and placed her chin on his midriff. 'Wow.'

'What?' He shifted his body to better accommodate her weight.

'Imagine seeing somebody else's reflection in the mirror. That's what this story is about. "Trapped souls."' She bent the page of the book she'd been reading, eyed the cover and plonked it down on his chest. 'What would you do?'

'Trapped what?'

'Souls. What if the reflection never moved? Stayed in your mirror forever? A kind of souvenir. Say if...'

'Any chance of a tea?' He felt much older than her; again. 'Two sugars please.'

'Christ, you're boring.' She sat up, shone the crummy light in his face. 'I need a fag. Why don't you smoke?'

'Um, why do you smoke?'

She was always like this afterwards. Very chatty; scared, he thought. Of course she's scared; she's 19 for God sake.

'Oh God, I need a fag. Can't you at least keep some here for when I come over?' She put emphasis on the word come and tweaked his nipple. Well that's what 19-year-olds do.

'Lend me a fiver. I'll get some from the BP garage up the road.'

'It's half past two.'

'That's okay, it's only Brixton. Come on, I'm gasping.'

He sighed, leaned over and opened his over-busy sock drawer. Stuffed down one side was a crumpled gob of cash that looked as if it had been laundered along with his underwear. He pulled out a bedraggled five pound note and launched it at her head.

'Cheers. You're a prince, baby.'

She sprung off the bed and searched for her underwear on the floor. He marvelled at her body as she dressed; lissom was the best way to describe her, or was it lithe; either way she was utterly stunning and 19. Fool.

She leaned over, kissed his cheek. 'Want anything?'

'A luger: two rounds.'

Shutting the bedroom door quietly, she was soon entering South London darkness.

'Flowers: um roses, um daisies, um begonias, um buttercups; lots of flowers must buy some for mum. No dad, no mum. Dandelions, snapdragons, sweet peas, um horse... something.'

She had seen him around. He was a street character: apparently harmless, always talking to himself. Persistent.

'Got a cigarette?'

'Sorry, don't smoke.'

'Where you going?' A childlike whining, as if she were an old friend who'd upset him. 'Where you going?'

'Petrol station.' Why did she tell him? Automatic. He followed close behind, mumbling.

'Another flower.'

'What?' Her pace quickened, as did his. 'Flower. Give me the name of a flower. To finish my collection.'

'Rose?' She replied quickly; breathless, unsteady.

'Got rose.'

The petrol station was on her right. Its greenish lights were reassuring. A huge, black 4x4 was leaving; music loud, sleek, hearse-like.

She approached the window of the station shop—they locked and barred the door after midnight for obvious reasons—and asked for ten Marlborough Lights. The man following her lurked by a gas pump, shuffled his feet, talked to something on the ground. The cashier eyed him with disdain as he slid the cigarettes under the plastic barrier with her change. 'You okay?' She nodded, but she didn't want to leave. Say if he wasn't harmless. She was pretty sure he lived in the sheltered accommodation at the end of the street. It wasn't far. How about if she walked that way, maybe he would go home?

She knew she could outrun him; well she was pretty sure she could, but why run? Wouldn't that agitate him?

She strode purposefully back towards the house, cigarettes gripped tightly in one hand. The 4x4 passed her and drove back into the garage; no music this time. Odd. Christ, she needed a fag.

'I thought you didn't smoke.'

The kettle whistled and split the early morning calm. It seemed to boil quicker in the early hours. He was sure that if he conducted an experiment he could prove this. But he could never be bothered. He poured the boiling water on to the coffee in the cafetiere. The smell was always wonderful. If only she were a bit more grown up. Was she even mature for a 19-year-old? Yes, she was smart; yes she was clever, but those moments when she was restless, childish; they drove him nuts. He stirred the coffee too vigorously. Some spilt over the glass spout and burnt his hand. He licked it and swore. After a minute or so, he pushed the lid down. Good, a strong one, tough to compress. He needed a strong coffee. She was exhausting; the randomness of her mind;

those daft questions. The story about the mirror business, trapped souls: how was he supposed to respond to her? He'd gone off fiction. Biographies and history books were what he read, now. Fiction was a waste of time.

He took a sip of the freshly poured coffee and looked at the pink clock above the kitchen window; ten past three. She'd been gone for half an hour. Odd. The garage was only up the road. He must have dropped off again after she'd left to get her fags. Where was she? He took another sip of coffee and walked to the front of the flat to see if he could spot her coming along the street. A night bus pulled up opposite his flat. Anybody on the top deck of a bus was at eye level with anybody who sat down at the window of his first floor flat. The top deck of this bus was empty. It stayed at the bus stop for a minute or so, rattled and hissed. For a moment he was hypnotised by the sound and forgot why he was staring out the window at ten past three on a Saturday morning. He felt like a father waiting for his errant daughter. Was she worth it? The only souls on the street were a group of lads, clubbers probably, milling outside the kebab house opposite. They were loud and were engaged in a chip fight. She was nowhere in sight.

Suddenly her little joke about Brixton didn't seem so funny. Yes, it was only Brixton, alright. He'd followed her out of the garage and up the road. Persistent.

'I thought you didn't smoke.' She thought about running again.

'I thought you didn't smoke.' He was closer now; stale tobacco and body odour. Turn around, kick him in the nuts; hard. Run, now. Give him a fag? 'Do you want one? They're not mine. They're for my husband. Do you want one?' She had slowed down and he was at her shoulder now.

'Yes please.'

She tore off the cellophane and threw it to the ground.

'You shouldn't do that. You should always put your litter in the bin. It's good manners.'

'Do you want a fucking cigarette or not, for Christ sake?' It was the depth of her voice that startled her, not the loudness. It came from deep down, shook her frame, felt strong. He felt it. She held the white and gold pack out towards him. Her hand shook violently. He took one. The transaction was awkward.

'Got any change?'

She pulled the change from the cigarettes out of her track suit bottom pocket and offered it to him. He took the change, counted the coins and dropped them into his back pocket.

'Got a light?'

She opened her dad's Zippo and flicked the wheel. He grabbed her shaking hand to ensure he lit the cigarette. She pulled her hand away easily and quickly and glared at him. She shook, but she was suddenly confident. She had the measure of him, she felt. She flicked the lighter to life again. This time he pushed his face towards the flame, cigarette protruding from his pursed lips. His head bobbed like a chicken as he sucked the cigarette into existence.

'Thanks. You shouldn't swear.' He walked off briskly, slightly hunched, hands in pockets, puffing the cigarette.

'Fucking cheek.' She smiled and sighed with relief, took the next right, stopped, and finally lit her cigarette. The 4x4 waited on the corner, humming, darkly watching.

The bus brakes startled him, woke him from his reverie. He'd been thinking about the first night he met her. Her energy had transfixed him then. She was vivacious and engaging. She wore an orange dress; retro and loud. The pub was noisy, but everybody heard her. She didn't shout, she just made people watch, listen. She knew about stuff: books and music; she was a

30-something in an 18-year-old body. Wasn't she? She held court with ease, made his friends laugh. Where was she?

He knew he had to go out. Brixton at half three in the morning. Great. He wandered back into the bedroom with his tepid coffee. The book she'd been reading sat on top of the crumpled sheets. He picked it up, sighed a laugh through his nostrils. The en-suite bathroom door stood ajar. He saw her headband on the floor and walked into the grey, murky light to pick it up. The flat was quiet, the chip fight had finished and only the occasional shush of wheels disturbed the peace. Brixton was almost silent. The headband was black with No Fear written in white. He crouched down and picked up the headband, fondled the soft, towelling material and smiled. Above him in the mirror was her reflection. She stood naked, lissom or was it lithe; either way, she was utterly stunning.

SADIE FROST
Dad's Nose

My dad's nose was a piece of sculpture
crafted out of other people's hands
where they'd hit and beaten it
in moments of anger.

A punch to punch his lights out!

A crack of flesh, a crunch of bone,
blood exploding down his face,
as his eyes lay unprotected.

His blue eyes twinkled with mischief,
tempting and seducing a slap;
tears and blood rolling together,
drying in a river of blood.

The first hit: 15 at school
by the playground bully.
Then at 20 and 2 years later.
And then again and again.

Doctors tried to rebuild it,
like the perfect sandcastle
that kids defiantly jumped on
and destroyed.

It never mended but sat sad and crumpled.
Redness and veins spidered his skin.

The famous nose looked carved from stone,
sandblasted to show angles of genius.

That was my dad's nose.

LUCIE BARÂT
Locked in

If you collected notches on your bed post, I collected hearts in a jar and kept my knickers on. And when I say 'collected,' I don't mean to imply that was a goal. It's not as if I stole; it's more as though they were abandoned on my door step, forced upon me. That's my side of the story, anyway.

It's not as though I cowered in the closet. It was more that stubborn boys kept booting me back in, shushing their lips and jamming their feet against the door. And I had no 'sistas,' I had few comrades to back me up. They'd just flick their eyes and agree with the boys, telling me lesbians don't have long hair, carry handbags, wear make up or dresses. Lesbians do NOT paint their fingernails or go to dance classes or leave behind them a trail of men.

COLIN MCKAY MILLER
The Next Thing to Go

You called last night.

I never know when you're going to call. I don't expect it, because it's so rare, but there was your number, unidentified as always. Most likely you stood at a payphone, calling card in hand, my number written on a scrap of paper I'm glad you still keep. I told you to come and meet me at my work today. You came, made jittery eye contact and said, 'Am I allowed to be in here?'

I forgave your wearing of that Cinderella shirt, because I know you have nothing left to choose. When I get close enough, you say, 'You might not want to hug me. I stink pretty bad.'

I do anyway.

I take a long lunch, tell my employer I'll be back sometime, and no one asks for clarification. I drive you back to my place, skip Bob Dylan's 'Like a Rolling Stone' because you know how it feels, and I trip enough conversation mines to keep the car moving in silence.

We've known each other too long to not know each other by now.

We eat sandwiches at the kitchen table. You're still opposed to rehab, convinced you're running from cops and family, and you tell me therapists always say the same thing. They talk to you like you're a little kid and medicate you. 'Antidepressants make you depressed,' you say. 'It's all a big scam. All of them should be banned.' You say antidepressants killed your mother. Effexor specifically. Time released pills released her from time.

You ask about your family, but I see them as much as you do. Stick a year-long planner up against the wall, blindfold me, and I'll chuck a dart to figure out when I'll see them next.

Glad to hear you're clean though. I know you didn't want to call when you were strung out. That's the best and worst moment—at a certain point you have to go in alone. You've been living out of your car for the last six months. Maybe that's why it keeps getting broken into.

We talk about the people you used to see. Wayne was a junkie you knew before he went to jail. He got mad at you one day, took your computer out to the dumpster with a 'free' sign stuck to it. By the time you traced it to another apartment, the hard drive was formatted; all your writing, all your work, gone. We admit the only reason you cared is because you wanted to be the one to get mad and destroy everything you've ever written.

Wayne's dead now. Another OD.

Wayne's girl, the Jag, turned him in and took over his apartment. (The Jag is named because of her resemblance to a certain Brit rocker.) The Jag painted a green stripe down the middle of one room and then went missing. I met her before she disappeared. It was a day when I dropped you off at that dirt apartment, empty 40s on the table, the radio blaring out of shut blinds. That Phil Collins track about how he saw a friend drowning and did nothing. It may be an urban myth, but I remember that was the tune.

The Jag opened the door, shot me one of the looks that said, *No sudden moves, mystery man.* If it had turned ugly, I would have shoved her in the pool. If the cops had shown up and asked why, I would have said, 'Because I'm the sober one.'

Better than getting an H needle spiked and snapped off in your vein.

We talk of Phil, the old guy who sent teenagers out in droves to buy Sudafed to make meth. There are better and faster ways, but now you hate meth, so no one's giving him any clues. People usually find meth labs in Colorado when they blow up— ah, there it is, under the flames—but you know you got lucky. Three more months in that neighborhood and you'd have been busted by the newly recruited task force—ninety-something stars pulled from all over the country, all working together to gut the local drug market.

Have I mentioned how happy I am that you're clean?

I ask you how many inspirational speeches you've heard lately and you put your head in your hands. 'Too many.'

I show you the shower, point out the lovely loofah, and say, heart all up in my eyes, 'Now give me a hug, you butthole.'

While you get cleaned up, I dig out all the promo toothbrushes I've received from the dentist. Those tooth scrapers always force them upon me. It's like they have an agenda or something.

I lift out the last of a twelve pack of 7 Up, a loaf of bread, granola bars, stuff you don't have to refrigerate. You said you want to get down to Manitou Springs for a chance to get it together near your doctor's office. We both know if you don't do something soon, you'll be dead in five years.

I'm making sure you go.

At first you leave the supplies in place. Finally I say, 'At least pick the money up off the table. You're making me feel like a blackjack dealer.'

You say you fried your brain pretty good, but you're more put together than the last time I saw you. Words come more easily, you look less like your mother, you're not writing your life with invisible ink. Still, you're hurt over lost love, the one you put everything in. I tell you that the ones that get away are supposed to get away, but you don't believe me. You'd like to find your ex in Washington one day, put the pieces of your separate lives together as one picture, but for now you're left with the fragments of 'Why couldn't we make this work?'

I know when to keep quiet.

It's good to see you, it really is. A long lunch is too short, but we rarely plan things outside of spontaneity. On the ride back, I give you one of my pens and tell you to pick up some spiral notebooks. That way, one day you'll be able to throw away everything you've ever written. I drop you back off at your car, let you drive off to anything, and I go back to my nice little job. I keep a face so quiet, people know not to ask. It's mostly an act, but sometimes it's nice to get what I want.

    You know what I want, right?

        I think you do.

12

Still like a sedated cow
Bluish tones blemish across
Frown lines and gritted teeth
Monotonous surprises stroke
The bare backed virgins
Drips of relief escape from
Gaping holes forming in
Machine like youth
Flung aside by
Over analysis
Questions fed to me
Like mush to a babe
Like rebellion to a teen
Crushed hopes
Uncrushable barriers
Dripping with the line
Punctured between
Pleasure and pain
Set fire to every muscle I can find
Yes yes
Even my own
Mainly my own
I have painted my hidden self
With unspeakable disgust
Don't come closer
I might scare you
I might be seen through.

DANNY McCOSH
New Year's Eve

It was New Year's Eve
and Johnny
staggered home.
He was paralytic,
but something caught his eye.
In a front garden
encased in a glass tank
was a beautiful Nativity Scene.
He stood entranced.
Then he opened the gate and stepped in.
He lifted his foot
And put a boot through the glass.
Using a shepherd as a truncheon,
He smashed all the figures to pieces
And ran
Laughing up the street
With the head of the Virgin
In His hand.

FEDERICA FREZZA
The Fool

Descending from the house seamlessly as an amphibious vehicle, he realized he had been drinking too much the night before. Maybe that's why it was so strange. Maybe it was just the most obvious explanation: he had drowned and no one had bothered to throw a life jacket his way—what a shameful thing.

He was so ashamed too, and yet, there was no one around who could be shocked by the disgraceful way he chose to be and to breathe and put one foot before the other at that slant rate that had the gall and the impudence not to rhyme. He trampled with strict precision each pool of rain. Were those tears? He had scattered them all over with the fear of not finding his way home.

She was dancing at the center of a square that looked familiar, as the clouds gathered over his head ready to explode in applause of thunder and lightning to the final pirouette.

In a dialogue with himself that moved him, he dropped all his aces and hoped for the best.

One that wasn't the same, that had been his until then, and that until then, had belonged to no one in particular, embraced him and called him back with sweet names before he obeyed as he would, were they a teacher and he a naughty schoolboy.

I've never heard the word reliable, he confided in her ear. I have. I'll tell you, he was told.

He melted into a golden lake, and when he emerged again, he was shiny and clean as a newly minted coin. He decided to spend himself saving nothing for darker days.

Snow and chocolate diamonds hovered over them in a wind rose, twenty-two windy concentric spirals rose. They argued for the bill, but his back was starting to ache, so he decided to let her win. So, it was that she went into the tank first, but the downpour was not enough to water all the flowers on the balcony. He had to tell a fascinating tale so that the tap would start pouring out sweet words again, and she was no longer cold.

It worked, as if he had changed the batteries.

A gust of air in two-four time opened the window like a landslide. Following the instincts of the animal she was, she threw herself on him to protect him. This was rewarded with an epidemic of kisses sealed in a bag with a red bow tied over backwards for that gesture so genuine it might as well play off as macrobiotic.

It was much later on, but sooner or later the wind from the convertible ruffled her hair and he knew that she was distracted. She was laughing so loud, sitting there on the side. Make it stop.

With a heavy suitcase loaded on his shoulders, he just rolled his eyes. It was a second, a second too late, a second time.

The silver handle went off like a faithful servant.

He saw her die, rolling like a single die that tumbled down the green plain of the slope, and focused on his prudent four-feet of rubber that never skidded on the edge of dangerous vortexes of stones and grass and continued on his way. He greeted the small mushroom growing next to his doorstep while he searched for keys (a minor b flat wolf-fifth) then one finally made it through the keyhole. The mushroom thought that his eyes were more numerous than normal.

The oranges rolled away as soon as he had crossed the bridge. He could never take them back from where he was now; he had never counted them after all.

What a liar, he who said the woman is fragile.

I want you to fuck me, she said, as soon as he managed to rip in tiny pieces the door that still separated them. And when she bit him, *touché* he cried. He was already wounded and the bleeding coagulated. Having nothing left in his pocket, not even a rabbit or a dove, he ran to school, so hopelessly late. There was no time for him; the courses had gone off course and they were already at the finishing line. He was left alone, just as in those days he had spent inside a tight and wet uterus, the rent for which was way too expensive.

She was laughing from the hillside and would never stop, not ever. He thought that nothing now could have put it right and chose to put it upside down, but fell into ruin, dislocating his wrist.

So defeated by the game, he sat on a stone and began to dry her hair, while a few tears began to slip from his fingers.

DAVE VEGAS
My Confession

I cry tears of vodka into dirty hands.

Almost despising my existence; fearing another day in hell, surrounded by the physical presence of many, but alone in my mind. The days go by and turn to weeks. Then weeks to months, until one day, as if by surprise, I try to remember a day before I was drunk or lavished with some kind of high—I can't remember that day.

I've lost everything, it's all just disappeared: home, relationships, job, possessions, dignity, sanity—life. And the more I lose, the less I want to regain. It's all just fallen through my fingers unnoticed, along with the sands of time. The thought and realisation of it all makes me feel dirty—a feeling which, if I'm truthful, I quite like. At least it's a feeling after all, right?

As I scrawl this confession into my beloved journal, I'm pouring vodka. These days it's as if I'm pouring it straight into my soul, just to kill the feelings of pain, regret and sadness. The mornings are the worst. The sobriety is deafening. It conjures feeling and thought, which is exactly what I spend the waking day trying to quell. I'm not one of those, however, that arise to vodka or reach for the half-empty can of Stella, which acted as my confidante the night before. I have to stick to the two tea rule, if only to cling to my last piece of sanity. Two cups of sugary tea before the booze. Besides, it staves off the hunger. It must be four or five days since I've eaten anything of substance. And, while I'm being honest, this was only to make sure I got the most from the inhumane quantity of speed I threw down my neck for dessert.

Amidst all my vices, the crazy thing is, no one seems to notice. Everyone looks, but no one sees. As a musician, a technically homeless musician at that, I see different people every day. Sleeping on different floors and sofas every night; everyone is willing to partake in this lifestyle for the odd time they spend with me, but fail to notice or do the same once I leave.

As I'm writing, I realise my biggest fear: the draining of people's kindness. What will I do once no one offers me a floor or sofa to kip on? When no one offers me one of the odd meals I'm able to force down? It's a thought I don't wish to carry on writing about at this point in time.

When I think of addiction, I think of someone sat behind closed doors, alone—hiding. Every night of the week, I'm either playing a gig, watching a gig or rehearsing—all of which feeds my dirty desire. In full, plain view of everybody watching. I've even overheard people excuse my actions as being creative. No one ever warns you about this kind of addiction, which is probably why, even now, I can justify it. In the beginning, it fuelled my writing and creative spirit; now I'm unsure. I mean, how would I know?

My biggest uncertainty is do I want to stop? What is there to go back to? I want to want there to be an end to this, but the 'want' just isn't there. Will I ever repair the gaping gashes in my life? Do I prefer them open? Will I ever heed my own call to live a normal life again? What is normal, if not a life measured by the ones that know no other way? So many questions, and I guess only time will tell. But I feel contented in the fact that, if it does happen, this—my confession—is the first step.

FRAN LOCK
Virgil Navigates Hell

It is a weary process, this.
The world wears its recovery
positions. Men
screwed in to foetal stations
balled mortals, facefirsting
the pavement
with violence, thirsting,
or on
their backs like beetles.
They sag, lug
up their *sweet Jaysuses*
like phlegm
on to the heatcrazed
concrete
of the dying day;
crawling,
bawling on the boiling bitumen,
twitching tweakers, jawing
in all of their ex-pat patter, their bullshit
banter, up out of themselves in their
trigger English:
It hurts to make sense.
It hurts.
It is a weary process, this.
They're writhing like dying
swans, caught up in sixpack
plastic.
I step between
the curb and their clutching, frantic
spastic hands, doing junkie gymnastics,
necks on springs and knees

like elastic, just snapping back and forth,
torqued contortionissimos, blowing little
kisses like slow wet raspberries.
These are my lovers,
the clotheared
dossers, bin- bagged, dropped
and dragged in to desperate postures,
drooling lolling lotus-eating, lost all feeling
in their legs.
Ponderously masculine,
skag-head dregs with
crusty dreads.
And they're speaking in tongues, seeking
in the tail-lights of taxies, love.
They're mothing between the bulbs
and I'm dancing,
surrounded by crashed
curved balls of names
I didn't catch;
they're just
a flash in a pan,
they're an itch
I can't scratch
like the crabs
in my snatch
Long John Goneagains
seized muscles ticcing
like roadkilled
corpses
and they trample
each other in the slapdash
scramble
for the stash, fumble

for cash
enacting
slow deaths
under a dull silver moon:
flat and white
as a wafer of host.
A ghost
like my face
cooking up
in the back
of a spoon.

JEROME ALEXANDRE
Drought Season

It's the closing hours of my birthday. I've blagged a tenner, some 'Hello Kitty' cake and a parting kiss from my mother. Although it's freezing outside, I have a mission. Running to the nearest train station, in this case, Maze Hill, I stand shivering on the platform. At this hour, trains are few and far between. I'm in a rush to score and I've still got to get to Deptford to collect some more cash from my step-dad. On arrival, I learn that my usual source has dried up.

It's drought season and every junkie has mournful intent in their eyes, like hounds without a fox to chase. I've always found South East to be colder than the North or West, emanating the kind of frost that relentlessly gnaws at your bones. Right now, I'm desperate for the warm, sharp distance that only heroin can bring. Gritting my teeth, I climb up the piss-stained stairs to my step-dad's place and he hands over my birthday bonus.

At New Cross Station, I call my friend Jack. At this moment in time, he's the only person in London able to get his hands on decent stuff. Unfortunately, he lives on the other side of town. Jack informs me that I'd better meet him in Putney, pretty darn sharpish. As any fool knows, getting to Putney from New Cross isn't easy in under an hour, but needs must, and Jack's King of The Hill, at least while his luck holds out.

The first lap of my journey is spent in an empty carriage, aside from a middle-aged African guy with startling orange hair wearing a tribal gown. He sits opposite me and starts waxing lyrical about JC and his suffering. On a good night, I'd be quite up for a debate, but picturing my mother's disappointment, I've plenty of guilt of my own, without having to add the Catholic variety to the morass of wrong-doings. Still, the preacher helps to pass the time and I miraculously get to London Bridge in ten minutes. The pathway to the Jubilee line is fraught with obstacles, including an immobile group of Japanese tourists who won't budge for shit. I'm the ball and they're the skittles, as I jump on to the tube. It's eight stops to Putney and we're moving at milk float speed, as if the driver has popped 20 Valium.

Finally at my destination, I realise I'm going to have to give up a pound of my scoring money to call Jack, which could fuck up my order, but better a phone call than no order at all. This adds stress and time and also requires having to get change at the ticket office, no easy task as there is only one guy at his station. He is being harangued by a commuter over a fine. 'Scuse me, this is urgent,' I yell, but no one hears me except a lovely old lady who gives me 60 pence for the call box. I pick up the receiver. 'Jack, I need three and two. Where are you?' I bleat. It's then that I hear the words that are the biggest kick in the balls. 'Sorry mate, we had to order without you, but there's someone else that will deliver.' This sends me into a frenzied panic. Who is this someone else? I've veered into unknown territory, which no junkie likes. I already know the substitute's gear will be nowhere near as good.

Fifteen minutes later, I stand sulking in Jack's front room. Smug and satisfied, Jack and his girlfriend, Lizzie, are blissed out on the sofa, smoking the finest crack known to humanity. Greedy as always, they inform me that their stash is not for sale and that there is a 45 minute wait for the substitute dealer. To fill the time, I take their dog, Lucky, for a walk. As I tremble and hold back puke, Lucky tugs me down to the riverside. Like his master, he feels like he can take the piss.

On the Thames, posh kids practice rowing, illuminated by blue beams. I fantasise about hijacking row boats, committing bloody murder and extracting fat wallets. Pulling the most maniacal grin I can muster, I gesticulate at the rowers but they don't respond in the way I anticipate. There is no horror, only jovial waves in my direction. I hate the wealthy for being as placid as the water they glide along on. It's all cheers and pats on the back for this lot. Like Lautremont's demonic character, Maldoror, who wishes misfortune on humanity, I long for the ship to capsize, drowning every wretch on board.

Jack, on the other hand, didn't need anyone to wish him ill. He's done it all by himself. Once a bassist for a Top 10 group, Jack had enjoyed a decent life until grave misfortune knocked on his door. Now a petty thief, he kept his nightmares at bay with heroin and crack cocaine. I guess this is what we had in common; we'd taken communion with success at an early age and lost it just as easily.

After an hour in the wild, I dragged Lucky home. My stomach felt like acid was swirling around it and my heart was hammering. I knocked on Jack's door. 'Is it here yet?' I asked. Jack nodded. Following him into the front room, I was more than ready to shoot up, however, any immediate release was blocked by a fat bloke injecting in his neck and chatting about *Top Gear* magazine. I wanted him to piss off so I could use in peace, and took refuge in the bathroom 'til he left.

'Is it any good?' I asked Jack. He shrugged and replied 'I only know as much as you.' He seemed vaguely irritated. How dare I puncture his high? I envied Jack's tranquillity, it had been awhile since I'd seen anyone gouch. Lizzie was slumped in a corner, equally zonked. God, I envied them, their temporary reprieve, numbed by the good stuff bought in my absence. I cooked the heroin and got the vein on the second go. I felt a mild warmth, but it was nowhere near the all encompassing caress that comes with a fine hit. Jack stood over me like I was a test case, watching for results. 'It looks like it's worked, your voice has dropped an octave.' He was trying to reassure me. 'Jack... it's garbage. The only decent stuff from this wretched drought is in front of you, on the table.' Lizzie interjected. In fact, interjecting was all that Lizzie did. 'Darling, we waited for you,' she slurred, 'But you were too long.'

I loaded some crack on the pipe, it was great, but without heroin to soften the rush, the high was too intense. This was as good as it was going to get. I was about to smoke my second rock when Jack said 'What about me and Lizzie?' Even though they both had plenty, they wanted some of mine for their so-called favour of calling in a dud substitute. On my last pipe, the gas ran out, destroying what little buzz there was; the rest burned into the ether. I shot the last two bags of heroin for double effect, but it wasn't much better. I had spent £50 and received no relief whatsoever. I could have wept. As I put my shoes on to leave, I realised that my feet were bleeding. I bid the gruesome twosome farewell, and limped home through back streets. Now would have been the ideal time to talk to the African man about Christ's suffering, the cross, and Calvary...

NINA ANTONIA
Sorry

I'm sorry I'm not the perfect daughter
I'm sorry I'm not the perfect mother
Perhaps if I was someone other
Than me
I'd look better
Talk better
Know better
Wouldn't flinch from criticism
Stand up tall and fight like a man
But I'm not good enough the way I am.
Too thin
Too fat
Out of sorts in my Mad Hatter's hat
Give me the rulebook
Tell me where to read
The recipe for harmony
Invisibility and anonymity
I'm not up to the mark
Don't make the grade
A poor deal for those who feel
Slighted, spited, disappointed
Thus anointed
I must be at fault
Deliver the wounds
Pass me the salt
Pale St. Sebastian
With the raspberry ripple chest
I used to be a martyr
Till I got a bullet proof vest

NADIA KHOMAMI
*** All Hallows Eve***

Drunk, lulled and restless I had drifted
Beneath a silent, idle sky, I sat and
Watched the night glide by with all its droll and
Dark delights.
But who would have thought that one night
I might have bumped into my end,
Into the barren fleets that hide
Within the crooked streets of
Lonely London's eastern end?

Who would have thought, that with leaking,
Worn out slack-jaws, their pale and creaking joints
And aches and the buds of my
Wine-stained mistakes would come
To suitably join laws. They said,

We are the moans that arise at dusk from that
Whore, that bitch, that London that screams,
That holy city that not once did pity the songs
We let loose into its streams, we are those that lie
Within its furies, deep, lost from excess of lust or lack
Of love and sleep,

Who here cares for our dead souls?

And I saw the tears that
Channel down the faces of all
These mad men of the street, and I felt the
Panic, the dread alarm of what happened
When their eyes and mine did meet.

My eyes that tore the mute sky apart, and all
My world that was sucked up into its heart, in
That splendid languor I finally did see
The brightest of all eternity, it put to bed battles
Between the drink in me, and all the dreams that
Did once sink in me.

I shouted all you of love,
And all you of warmness, you that screen
And point behind your harness,
Board up your windows, your children need not
See all this trembling cold, and colder fear
Set free. Save the children, just
Save them all. And

In the undertow were we then caught,
The grim and grotty dwellers of your fright, went
Rolling on down Saint Arthur's Street and
Plunging into a bottomless night,
Swept up off your pavements and off your
Dawnings, off your bright and clear
Cut winter mornings.

We the stabs, the scabs, the sex and silent specks
Of distant stars, we the perverts,
Prostitutes and punch, the louder, loudest
And hardest bunch of fiends you'll
Ever meet,
We that forage, we the national debt, we
The hate and grubby brushed off dirt, the
Unruly cowards, the barbarians, the banished
And accursed,

Who here cares for our dead souls?

Drunk, lulled and restless I had drifted
Beneath a silent, idle sky, I sat and
Watched the night glide by with all its droll and
Dark delights.
But who would have thought that one night
I might have bumped into my end,
Into the barren fleets that hide
Within the crooked streets of
Lonely London's eastern end?

Now I am that moan that arises at dusk, from
That whore, that bitch, that London that screams, the
Holy city that not once does pity the songs
I let loose into its streams.

Who here cares for my dead soul?

CIARA BURKE
Libertine

And Midnight's pissed with cheap champagne
and 10p plastic cups, we're sprawled across
the lawn with our hearts hanging out.
All that's in my mind is contempt
for everything and nothing, my fingers
in my ears to block out the shouting
and she's dripping her life into me
and I have no will to stop her so
I plug my fingers in my ears.
And with the fucking food poisoning
and the wrecked guitars, all we've
got is a hope that tomorrow might
be better, and maybe we might get there.

And Midday's fucked on cheap cocaine
and 10p condoms, thrown across the lawn.
Same old places we left behind and same
old faces we'll never forget, cause we
can't really, it's what we are. And
she just looks at me and cries, but
what's the point of tears in this big
city, where every day a baby dies and
another writer drops off the face of the
earth, too hard, too hot and just aching
for the passion he left in his fucked up home.
And he's throwing up in the elevator, a
needle hanging off his arm; despair.

And Andy's screwed with five pound notes
stuffed up her nose, licking the final
chalky spots off her fingers, bloody knees

from where she acted like a drag queen on
the concrete steps. And I have more than
enough four letter words to describe this place
and its white walls we can't afford to paint.
You think its all about romance and ecstasy
when you're a kid; you just ache for the day
you fuck off into your dream; but in the end
no matter where you go you still have the
same headaches. We're all lost children,
we don't have no parents and we never grow up.

But Midnight's high on childish dreams and
glazy eyes that wished for a better world.
I'm dribbling romantic poetry waiting for
my life to take hold. Maybe this is life and
maybe we, me and Andy, maybe we have it made.
I've got ambition and I've got imagination.
I imagine a city with four drunk boys walking
with guitars and I imagine a girl with hair
you couldn't even dream of wrapped around my fingers.
And it's all parody, a parody of songs about
true love and rock n roll. And maybe with our
cheap champagne it's brighter here than anywhere else
and maybe we've got it fucking made.

COLLEEN ALLEN
RIP

I am writing a letter to a man
It's a virtual offering
it sits in the ether
my papyrus & carrier dove
this is special
it carry-eth not my love.
And I can't put a 'pen' to 'paper'
So I screw it up and try it all over again
and it hurts like bereavement,
over and over and over again
like a knife
as it catches my craw
and it sticks in my throat
It rages adrenalin
shots in my heart
hurt like bereavement
and this was before you died
No parole or benevolent leave
from the scars that won't heal
keloid handcuffed and ultimate deal
is that never
ever
ever
will you know
or feel
how I feel.
You were my God
And then I died
Slow and deliberate
a murder
Not one with blood spill

or chalk marks or strange pills-
Not yet, anyway.
This body remained
mostly un-tampered
But the spirit
she dipped
she tripped
and cantered
downwards
to your
special
devil
hell
Every day I tried
So hard
my thinking muscles
twisted their neuron hands in strain
With my small self
and young silly ways in vain
to make you a tiny bit proud
But the truth was you noticed me not
Not a bit
not a lot
not a jot
From baby to toddler to infantile
I limped through the ages with limited smiles
With head bowed and tongue tied and eyes dull and
arms wide
For reciprocating love that I never had possession
And you didn't feel me worthy of a place in your world
Though you stole me from another and left me dormant
And you used me for your exorcism used me for
torment

All my best drawn like a vile osmosis
Drawn through a straw and replaced with neurosis
I was 9 years old when you broke me like a whore
Only valid or use to fuel your raging head war
You gave me a vocabulary worthy of the scum
heads – you hated with passion that were dirt beneath your foot
treads – mercilessly over all my natural urge to kindness
Feeding me with bigotry and hate and social blindness
I mouthed out all your words to my mother that were spoon fed
Tasting like poison I spat them through the phone – red
The colour of the blood that you threatened to spill
when you held out the knife that was angled to kill
on your wrists translucent, your eyes of blue chill
Alcoholic calm drunk
Filthy cocktail vein junk
Lobotomised to head funk
ECT and brain krunk
Poor Daddy
Where art thou now?

ANNA KIRK
Wholesome

The question is, can one person
be all four Beatles?
(The other question is, can one person
be another's everything?)

I used to be two, but now I am one.
This is the opposite of loneliness.
My shoulders no longer bear
the thing that crouched.

EILIDH MACDONALD
Self Portrait at the Lowry

Not here, the dramatic charcoal buffetings of a storm in Galilee;
No monstrous waves of inky despair, no salt-bitter flecks
Of phosphorescent spume upset a vessel
Engorged and radiant in disaster. No blistering strokes howl doubt across the page,
No green-tinged, sunken face glares desperately to the sky,
No glowing muscles writhe in enraged national monument;
There is no dark, grasping scramble for a better place.
Half-remembered guilt does not surface from an oily scratch to wash, blackly,
Through a golden frame and claim redemption on the burning horizon.

Here drifts the pencilled terror of calm, flat tides
Unfolding their cold certainty in passing minds;
Never breaking ripples that will blankly die,
Their pale moment fading to an endless, longing smudge;
Never touching anyone.

ISAAC JAMES BAKER
This is Gregory Sampson

I am Gregory Sampson. This is Gregory Sampson.

In the past six months, Gregory Sampson has ordered 64 grande lattes from Vicky, the barista at the Starbucks on Dupont Circle North. Each time he is charged $3.49, plus the applicable 10 percent Washington, D.C., sales tax. Vicky is 28, one year older than Gregory Sampson. But Gregory Sampson does not know this yet. He does not know much of anything about her at this point besides her name and current occupation. This is because Gregory Sampson has only gathered the courage to ask her one question: 'Can I get an extra shot of espresso?'

Gregory Sampson's mother calls him on Sunday mornings. She does this because she feels responsible and guilty that her only son doesn't attend church. Gregory Sampson knows she listens closely to his tone in an attempt to determine how drunk he was the previous evening.

This is what Sister Martha writes on a 9-year-old Gregory Sampson's first quarter report card: 'Gregory is such a pleasure to have in class.'

Gregory Sampson has been working on his first novel for ten months. It is about a spaceship manned by chimpanzees that enters a black hole. But no matter how many books or scientific journals he reads, Gregory Sampson cannot grasp the theory or the physics of black holes. They confound him. He finds himself depressed, drinking too much coffee, and gnawing at his nails every time he sits down to work on his novel.

This is what a 9-year-old Gregory Sampson says when Father McClellan puts his hand down Gregory Sampson's pants for the first time: 'Please don't.'

The bus Gregory Sampson takes to Dupont Circle is the L2. While en route, Gregory Sampson passes three Starbucks establishments, each of which serve perfectly adequate lattes. If he were to buy his lattes from the Starbucks in Woodley Park, which is a two-minute walk from his apartment, he would save an average of six dollars a week in bus fare. When Vicky is not on duty, Gregory Sampson goes without his hot, caffeinated beverage. Gregory Sampson does not even particularly like grande lattes. He does, however, like the way Vicky calls out his order as she places his cup on the bar.

This is the working title of Gregory Sampson's first novel: *Chimps Lost in Space.*

When Gregory Sampson is 14, he asks his high school girlfriend, Summer Truman, the following question during their third time having sexual intercourse: 'Can I stick it in your bum?' Summer Truman replies thusly: 'Who says 'bum' anymore? What are you British or something?'

Vicky has the following last name: Bertucci. Gregory Sampson becomes aware of this fact as he watches Vicky steam the milk for his latte, the 68th one she's made for him. This is how he finally introduces himself: 'I'm Gregory. Gregory Sampson.' Gregory Sampson finally gathers the courage to ask her a question that is not directly related to a Starbucks beverage. Here is what he asks: 'Would you like to go out for a cup of coffee sometime?' Gregory Sampson, upon speaking these words, realizes how ridiculous he must sound to Vicky, as she is currently on the clock at Starbucks, the world's most famous purveyor of coffee.

This is when Vicky Bertucci gets off of work at Starbucks that evening: 6:30 p.m. This is what Gregory Sampson says after Vicky Bertucci tells him this fact: 'Well, I'm free. Would you like to get some pizza?' Vicky Bertucci says the following: 'Pizza would be a lot better than coffee!' As she says this, Gregory Sampson decides Vicky Bertucci's baby blue eyes are the prettiest things he's ever seen.

This is what Gregory Sampson's mother asks a 9-year-old Gregory Sampson the night Father McClellan first rapes him: 'Would you like to stop at Baskin Robbins on the way home?' This is what a 9-year-old Gregory Sampson says in reply: nothing.

If Gregory Sampson ever publishes *Chimps Lost in Space* he will likely face a lawsuit on the grounds of copyright infringement from the company that owns the rights to *Lost in Space*, the tremendously popular 1970s television series, and the copyright owner of the not-so-popular 1998 theatrical film of the same name.

On their first date, Vicky Bertucci orders the following dish at Pizze, a rustic Italian eatery in the Woodley Park neighborhood: a personal Hawaiian pizza. This is what Gregory Sampson says to Vicky Bertucci from across the table: 'Good choice!' This is what Vicky Bertucci says after Gregory Sampson orders a personal pizza with onion and anchovies: 'You're a brave man.'

This is what Father McClellan preaches from the pulpit the Sunday after he first rapes Gregory Sampson: 'His eyes are on the sparrow. And He watches over me.'

This is the film Gregory Sampson and Vicky Bertucci watch after eating their personal pizzas from Pizze: *The Departed*. This is how many bottles of wine Gregory Sampson and Vicky Bertucci consume at Gregory Sampson's apartment while watching the film: two and a half. Here is where they go together after shutting the movie off just before the bloody dénouement: Gregory Sampson's bed. Here is what Gregory Sampson tells Vicky Bertucci briefly after climaxing inside her: 'Oh, my God...'

Here is what Gregory Sampson names the chimpanzee captain of the ship in *Chimps Lost in Space*, the working title of the novel he is currently not writing: David Greybeard. This is because David Greybeard is the only name of a chimp he knows and he is too lazy to come up with another name. David Greybeard rises to popular knowledge because primatologist Jane Goodall studies this chimpanzee in his Tanzanian jungle habitat for many years. David Greybeard is quite likely the most famous chimpanzee in history, a fact that will surely confuse many readers of his novel, should it ever be published.

When a 10-year-old Gregory Sampson says he no longer wishes to go to mass or confession, this is what his mother says: 'God will forgive you for your rebellious desires. But as long as you are in my house you will attend mass regularly. Father McClellan would agree with me.'

This is what Sister Martha writes on a 10-year-old Gregory Sampson's first quarter report card: 'Gregory seems to have lost all interest in his school subjects. I have attempted to speak with him about his sloppy homework assignments, the way he falls asleep in class or just stares out the window all the time. However, Gregory remains unresponsive to the point of being disrespectful and disruptive. Forgive me for asking, but is everything alright at home?'

Here is what Gregory Sampson's friend Anne Brandenburger says upon hearing that he had sex with Vicky Bertucci for approximately six hours on their first night together: 'You guys go and shack up on the first date? Damn! Six hours?' Gregory Sampson replies thusly: 'Who says 'shack up' anymore? What are you, my mother?' Here is what Anne Brandenburger says to Gregory Sampson in reply: 'No, I'm not your mother. I don't call you all the time to make sure you're taking your vitamins and going to confession.'

This is who Gregory Sampson tells about Father McClellan raping him 78 times over the course of two years: no one.

A 14-year-old Gregory Sampson never gets to 'stick it' in Summer Truman's 'bum.' She tells him it would make her feel like Gregory Sampson is a 'fag or something.' Upon hearing this reaction from Summer Truman, a 14-year-old Gregory Sampson says the following: 'Father McClellan's a fag. I'm not a fucking fag!' Summer Truman replies thusly: 'Who's Father McClellan? And what the hell does he have to do with anything?'

This is how much Vicky Bertucci charges Gregory Sampson for his 71st grande latte from the Starbucks on Dupont Circle North: $0. She says the following in a sexually charged voice as she slides his beverage across the bar: 'You can pay me back later.'

In his research for *Chimps Lost in Space*, Gregory Sampson frequently consults the work of Jane Goodall. The following passage, which he stumbles across while waiting for the L2 bus, strikes him deeply: 'I have observed chimpanzees hugging, kissing, patting each other on the back and even tickling each other. These gestures are evidence of the close, supportive, affectionate bonds that develop between family members and other individuals within a community, which can persist throughout a lifespan of more than 50 years.'

'No way!' This is what Vicky Bertucci says upon hearing that Gregory Sampson's favorite film of all time is the 1970s classic *Midnight Cowboy*. 'I can't watch that movie without crying. Rizzo, he breaks my heart every time.' Gregory Sampson puts his arm around her following this comment. This is what Gregory Sampson says to Vicky Bertucci in his best New York accent: 'I'm walking here! I'm walking here!'

Enrico 'Ratso' Rizzo is played by the following Oscar-award-winning actor: Dustin Hoffman. Vicky Bertucci tells Gregory Sampson that he is much better looking than Dustin Hoffman. 'Even *The Graduate* Dustin Hoffman?' Gregory Sampson asks. Vicky Bertucci says the following in reply: 'Yes.'

This is what Gregory Sampson's father dies of: lung cancer. He is 49. This is what an 11-year-old Gregory Sampson says when his mother tells him the news of his father's death: nothing.

Gregory Sampson considers himself an agnostic, but sometimes he prays aloud when he is drunk in his Woodley Park apartment. This is what he prays: 'Lord, or whoever you are, what the hell is going on down here?'

This is what Father McClellan says to a 10-year-old Gregory Sampson after he catches him ditching church to play soccer with some neighborhood kids: 'I always knew you'd turn out to be a fuck-up.'

This is what Gregory Sampson thinks after he finishes reading Steven Hawking's book *A Brief History of Time* for the third time: 'I still don't know a damned thing about black holes.'

This is who an 11-year-old Gregory Sampson's mother asks to lead the funeral ceremony for Gregory Sampson's father: Father McClellan.

Father McClellan says the following during the funeral for an 11-year-old Gregory Sampson's father: 'He was a man of the Lord, a man after my own heart.' This is what an 11-year-old Gregory Sampson says to Father McClellan following the funeral ceremony: 'If you ever mention my father again, I will cut out your heart and shove it down your throat.'

This is how many times Father McClellan puts his hands down Gregory Sampson's pants after this conversation: none.

Here is what Gregory Sampson reads in *Nature*, a reputable scientific journal, as he is doing research for his failed novel: 'To solidify their positions of dominance, alpha males will frequently masturbate and ejaculate into the mouths of other lower-ranking chimpanzees.' This is what Gregory Sampson writes in the outline of his novel after reading this startling fact: 'There's no way Captain David Graybeard is going to jack off in the other space chimps' faces. Even if it's realistic, it's not happening in my novel.'

This is what Gregory Sampson's mother says when she reaches him on his lunch break Friday: 'You should come back home for the long weekend. Father McClellan passed away a few days ago. His funeral is Sunday. It would mean a lot if you could come home and honor him.' This is what Gregory Sampson says in reply: 'I'm busy this weekend, Ma.' Gregory Sampson's mother asks the following question: 'What could be more important than honoring a man of God? A man who tried to show you the love of our Lord?'

Love: this is the word Gregory Sampson says to himself over and over in his mind.

This is who Vicky Bertucci texts William Shakespeare's 116th sonnet to while she is working at Starbucks on Monday afternoon: Gregory Sampson. Here is how Shakespeare's 116th sonnet starts: 'Let me not to the marriage of true minds/ Admit impediments. Love is not love/ Which alters when it alteration finds...' This is what Gregory Sampson says upon reading William Shakespeare's 116th sonnet on his cellular phone: 'Damn. That's beautiful.'

Gregory Sampson's mother calls him on Monday evening and says the following: 'Have you heard about these horrible allegations of abuse against Father McClellan? Surfacing after his death? How terrible! Some half-wit from the neighborhood is going around spreading this impossible nonsense. Why would someone want to ruin the legacy of such a wonderful man of God with these lies? Gregory, are you getting enough vitamin C?'

This is how many milligrams of vitamin C the United States' National Academy of Sciences recommends an adult male should consume daily: 60 to 90. This is how much vitamin C Gregory Sampson gets on average: 155% of the daily recommended intake.

Gregory Sampson thinks the following as he stares out at the National Cathedral from the fifth-floor rooftop of his Woodley Park apartment complex Tuesday morning: 'How is it that I can have something so beautiful when I've been through something so horrible?' At that moment, Gregory Sampson decides to tell Vicky Bertucci about Father McClellan.

'I want to say 'I'm so sorry,' but that would just sound like bullshit.' This is what Vicky Bertucci says after Gregory Sampson tells her he was sexually abused by his priest for two years. This is what she says next: 'I don't know what to say.'

Here is what Gregory Sampson says in reply: 'You don't have to say anything.'

This is what Vicky Bertucci says in reply: 'I love you.'

Here is what Gregory Sampson does after Vicky Bertucci wipes the tears from his cheek: kisses her softly on the lips.

Gregory Sampson decides to abandon his novel about Captain Graybeard, *Chimps Lost in Space*. He chooses instead to start a novel about a young man, abused by a priest when he was young, who falls hopelessly in love with a woman in a coffee shop. The working title of this novel is this: *You Don't Have to Say Anything*. This is the basic theme of the book: together, two wounded people who love each other are stronger than they could have ever been alone. Given industry statistics, it is extremely likely this novel will never be published.

However, if *You Don't Have to Say Anything* does see publication, this is what Gregory Sampson will write on the dedication page: 'For Father McClellan.'

I am Gregory Sampson. This is Gregory Sampson.

DOMINIC STEVENSON
The Person Opposite on the Train

You know we'll wed
And live 'til we're dead
Because you caught my eye
On the 16.42 from Vauxhall.
You know that one day
We'll tell our friends about me
Just making it through a closing door
To the carriage,
Where you'd been waiting
For me,
All of your life.
Each night we will thank
The 8.3% of South West Trains that are delayed,
Then cuddle.
Except I didn't get through
The closing doors
Because as I ran up the stairs,
Towards you
My love
Who I never knew,
My wife called.

JACK VARNELL / THE EMOTIONAL ORPHAN
Flashes

I wonder what will flash before me
falling towards the ground
faster than the thoughts coming now.
What will the slow motion
instant replay be as the
blood melts with, equals, and
finally outweighs the bathwater.
Will final thoughts even register
as hammer strikes brass and
the smell of smoke
and gunpowder is announced.
Regret, fear, accomplishment, failure.
Good, bad, or ugly, or
no thoughts at all.
Logic does not exist for me
or I wouldn't be contemplating this.

NINA ANTONIA
The End of the World Is Nice

I hate fresh faces. Unblemished, no brow furrowed, soft lips plump with memories of mother's milk, satisfied and compliant. TV teens with silken hair and sun kissed bodies, luscious yet insipid. Where's the corruption that makes people interesting? I loathe this nicotine-fearing, low-calorie world of inane perfection; holidaying adults, Roman Gods without the blood. Drug-free festival children marvel at Nokia mirage; fists raised to the sky, saluting nothing but their own participation in the beautiful mass. The end of the world is nice.

I pine for the beauty of cigarettes, imperfection, decay, insalubrious basements and the forgotten joy of character: lunatics, unsung poets, bitten nails.

I renounce Kindle and the kunt who kreated it. Who would want a book without pages, creases, age, none of experience's imprint? Folks who go mall shopping, imbibers of the homogenised, watchers of the X Factor, deep-sleepers. The grubby pleasure of a cheap paperback with a seamy broad on the cover, promising the forbidden, is already a lost art. When all taboo is forgiven, what's left?

My man is a roller derby; he's a sparks flying, smashing into crash barriers kind of guy. I like his scars and bruises. Give me a hard-bitten gangster's moll with a Novocaine smile, a wolfish rogue, a done-in dolly bird, the loner from number 12, all of life's curios. Even vampires have been sullied, reeking now, not of the crypt, but designer aftershave and acceptance. Poe and the conqueror worm have been rendered obsolete by fresh faces.

Once I crawled under night's vast tarpaulin in search of unknown tributaries, like a kid sneaking into the circus, but all I found was the chattering locusts of addiction. Craving is the great equaliser, where model and maniac raise a pipe to eternal futility. At least it was some kind of real. Hail the shoplifter, capitalism's silent spoiler; every little bit helps. Perversity comes at the end of a journey, misspent.

I want those fresh faces to crack and fall like scrambled eggs. Washed up on life's crags where the rest of us flail. Don't tell me your daddy doesn't love you when he still pays the bills. Relocation, relocation, relocation. Who are these couples with a townhouse and one in the country, ushered into endless, delicious, palatial rooms? Beyond television, do these moneyed folks exist? They give birth to more fresh faces. Pain-free, of course.

JACK COOPER
Upstairs

Everything smelt of rubber.
Twenty metres up the road it stopped.
There was a small sofa, which we never sat on.
He put on gloves and pulled up his hood,
crouching on the floor in
pre-fix urgency.
I watched the whole scene in a rear-view mirror.
Old works, cups of cloudy water,
pieces of bloodstained tissue.
With cars in gear, there was a smash.
As Cohen prepared for a hit and shaking tried
for a vein.
The alarm sounded:
Knowing there's crack in the pin,
he didn't even lean in. He erupted into a
fullblown sprint.
It'll do that to you.

LUCIE BARÂT
Me, twice

I caught a butterfly when I was nine years old. It had flown in through my bedroom window and was fluttering around the pane, trying to find its way out. I put it inside a silk purse that I'd been given for my birthday and went downstairs to eat my tea. Dad always had the radio on while we ate. We had to be quiet so he could listen to the shipping report, even though the nearest coast was a good hour's drive away and we didn't own a boat. I put a mound of mashed potato on my fork and pressed in two green pea eyes. I waddled the fork over to a pool of tomato ketchup and dunked it several times, head first, until the potato-mound-man was bleeding profusely. My mother clipped me around the back of the head and my older sister let her eyes roll down my face in disapproval.

Jenny, from next door, came to knock and we spent the evening playing in the street until the summer light began to fade and the birds started tweeting in response to the curfew. We squealed and chatted with the other children who were allowed out after tea. Tiffany Chaplin brought two pilfered Custard Creams from her kitchen. We huddled into a conspiratory circle, passing the biscuits around and taking a nibble each. Tiffany bit off the biggest crumbs and declared the biscuit circle 'girls only.' The dusk came quickly and brought a cool freshness with it. Our noses started to drip and we disappeared, one by one, as our names were bellowed from various doorsteps. Jenny and I were the last. We left the chalk outlines of wonky hopscotches and smiley faces on the pavement behind us.

I am the youngest of three and therefore spent my childhood in lukewarm, third-hand baths. It was either that or share with my sister and I preferred chilly solitude. I used to stare at my reflection in the mirror. I'd focus on my pupils and let everything else go fuzzy and fade out. I used to look for the 'real me.' I wanted to know what I looked like without the childish features. I wanted to know what other possibilities were inside me. I slid my pre-pubescent body into the tub and huddled my knees to my chest, picking at a scab on my leg. I pulled off the brown crust and released a little slow-running rivulet of bright-red blood. I dripped water onto it to make it run further. Then I let myself lie back and dipped my head under the scummy water, practising, in case I ever had to drown. I let the water invade my ears and nose. I let out air in wobbly bubbles that lolloped to the surface. I opened my mouth just as my head shot up, involuntarily, to the chilly air of our bathroom, gasping and coughing.

Little goosebumps paraded down my arms, proudly displaying little blonde hairs like battlefield banners, ready to fight the cold. I felt my lips quiver and my stomach muscles tighten. But I stayed sat in the tub, practising, in case I ever had to freeze to death. Eventually, I got out of the bath and pulled the plug. My mother pounded on the door for me to hurry up. I ignored her and stole some of my sister's talcum powder that she'd managed to save since Christmas. I brushed my teeth and avoided looking at my reflection in the mirror. My mother pounded on the door again. I pulled on my nightie and it stuck to my body, creating a nylon force field.

I said my goodnights and climbed the stairs to my bedroom, shutting the door behind me. Dad had bought energy saving light bulbs and they always took ages to flicker on and warm up. I stood by the door, forcing myself to adjust to the dark and then the dim half-light. I stayed frozen until the light had found its feet and it was safe to cross the room.

I knelt on my bed and leaned on the window sill, as though I were praying, and carefully opened the purse. The butterfly was motionless and shrivelled. It had a cluster of tiny little eggs around its abdomen. I threw the insect corpse out of the window and watched the purple silk of the purse fall between the branches of the neighbours' privet hedge. I got up from my bed and stared at the pupils of my eyes in the wardrobe mirror. I wanted to know who was in there, underneath the blonde curls and pink skin. I knew there was someone desperate, someone I'd have to watch.

KJERSTI FURU
I Got A Balinese Dancing Girl Tattooed Across My Chest

    i keep writing my name down so as to not forget who i am. i want to exist when i'm not here. i will keep running in circles trying to catch the last person i slept with, the last person to look at me in a crowded room. look at me again. look at me again and again and again. and i will keep asking, never stopping for one moment, to hear the answer. i am the girl with a jar full of coppers and a laugh not fuelled by drugs. i am the girl i left crying in the street at 5 a.m. i am the girl who can't decide where she should be, and thus can never be the first to leave. i am the girl you will remember when she's gone. look at me. white knuckles adorning the glass. repeat. repeat. repeat.

DANNY McCOSH
Bowing Out in Bow

High in your flat
In that block in Bow
The first place I ate roasted vegetables
It was spacious
And you loved us to come around
We drank
Talked
Partied
And parted for the disco
Records spinning
Us all singing
You were beautiful
Quite fanciable
Mixed race—black and white and Bow
We were kindred with our East End and Essex twangs.
This was all Heaven
But we didn't know that things change.

One day in the deepest despair
You heaved your body over the balcony—
Dead—
We were gobsmacked
—Onto the pavement below.

FRAN LOCK
Feme Sole

I am not aging.
I gestate a decay.
Keep away. Leave me
communing with God.
A one-sided conversation
like a prison visit.
I was a convent child, stored
in the stewing gloom
of a two storey schoolhouse. I shared
the sickly complicity of little girls
with the saints and their vocabulary
of wounds.
This is not my world.
You hang Christ on the cross
with clothes pegs to dry.
I am not like you.
I dream. I see
my shroud,
wrapping me tight
as a fish-supper.
I dream. I see
my mother cross
the threshold
of a convalescent silence.
She recover from me
as from a long illness.
But I am not ill.
I distill my decay
like *poitín*. Keep away.
It is not your darkness I seek.
The white walls redouble

the daylight and fill
the oblong space behind my head
with a brightness
like a near death experience.

RHIANNON WILLIAMS
A Letter to My Little Brother

I do not remember the diagnosis. I remember tears, and trips down south to see doctors and specialists, and mum crying at the kitchen table when I came in from school. I remember all these things. But if I try and pinpoint a moment where I went from knowing to not knowing, I find that I can't. It's like stretching my fingers out wide and then clenching them tight, only to find them frustratingly empty. You can't pocket air. That memory is will-o'-the wisp, glowing in the darkness, luring me nowhere at all.

I want to write something beautiful about you. I want it to be poetic, and literary, and harrowing. I want sophisticated prose. I want people to marvel at the elegant turn of phrase, to cry at the sad parts and laugh at the good parts, to understand, to empathise and identify. But it just doesn't work when I try; it comes out as self-pitying, or affected, or it trivialises you or does you wrong, and the person on the page is not you, suddenly, but a stranger, a medical case, a crusade. So I am writing this to you, instead, although I'm not sure you can read, and there are no pictures here for you to label, triumphant that your mouth is making sounds that other people understand. It's all about feelings, really, and I know that you struggle with those. I'm sorry for that.

They thought that you might have something worse. That you wouldn't live to see your teens. It might have come as a relief, then, the actual diagnosis, I don't know, because I can't remember. I remember you.

I remember chubby fingers, and woolly jumpers. Long walks by the lake, and even longer eyelashes. Blowing bubbles, your Spiderman pyjamas, gappy teeth. I remember looking at other children in playgrounds and thinking: 'they are fine.' I wanted you to be fine, too. I remember you blowing out your birthday candles for the first time ever. We were so proud. You were ten.

And sometimes I dream about you. We are children again, and you are small, and blond, with your hamster cheeks and your big, blue, empty eyes. You were such a beautiful baby. You are clutching my hand and I am leading you somewhere, but then you evaporate and I am alone, and something inside, some still, small voice tells me that you are dead. When I awake, it is with big choking sobs, and I know that I will not be doing anything or going anywhere, today.

So I could talk about the crying in my sleep, or the tears, or the tantrums, or the shit on the floor, because of course, I remember them too. I won't, though. These things didn't make the house any less empty for mum when you left. I hope you didn't think that we gave up on you. I think she worried about that; she felt guilty for not being able to look after you any more. But she did—wonderfully, don't you think? You just got too big and strong.

I remember when you were six and Dad moved out and you used to sleep in your shoes and your coat, just in case he came in the night to get you. You wouldn't let mum take them off. And you used to say 'daddy, daddy, daddy' over and over and over. It would drive us mad, but it also broke our hearts. And when you cried, it was the saddest thing that I have ever known. Your eyes would fill up and your bottom lip would tremble, and you would howl. How you would howl. Boys aren't usually allowed to sob; I don't think Dad has ever cried like that.

He didn't leave you, though. I hope you know that. He is just a lot like you. Not good with feelings and stuff. We all miss you, all the time, every day. I miss when you were little and you used to come and wake me up, and you would snuggle in next to me and laugh. And I miss your pink elephant wellingtons boots, and your hair being all different lengths because you wouldn't sit still when mum cut it, although you're just as handsome now. I didn't know that I could love so much until we had you. It's not just because you're vulnerable, that you need protecting. I think it's also because you can't show you love me back, you don't know how. So I have to do it for both of us.

I do not remember the diagnosis, but I do remember you: on the bank of the lake, in your red coat, your wellington boots, throwing stones. My baby brother. In all your chaotic, speechless, detached loveliness; I remember you.

MICHAELA TURNER
A Riddle

My first is in teacher, but not in pet
My second's in teeter, but not in regret

My third is in under, but never in stated
My fourth is in over, but never in rated

My fifth is in bud, but not in darling
My sixth is in spitting and shouting and snarling

My seventh's in spinster and also in lodger
My eighth's in spiteful and artful and dodger

My ninth is in proper, but not in property
My tenth is in mirror, but not in mockery

My eleventh's in death, but not in duty
My twelfth's in truth, but not in beauty

My whole is in one night
But cannot quite stand
The thought of the daylight
The clammy minute hand.

Who am I?

EMMA JONES
Tell Me About Your Father

A support group for people with various mental health problems. The group runs once a week and is a preparatory group before the main treatment programme. People drift in, grab tea, have a quick ciggie.

INT: Community Hall
ADAM, professional therapist, 40s, facilitates the group.
SANDRA, 50s, severe borderline personality disorder.
AMY early 30s, post-traumatic stress.
DAVID, late 30s, middle-class, anxiety.
MOHAMMED, 40s, from Liverpool, dissociative disorder.
JUDY, mid-30s, anxiety and anger issues.
JANINE, early 20s, anxiety, panic attacks.
STEVE, 40s, anger issues.

ADAM (To group)
Good morning!

SANDRA
Is it?

AMY (To Sandra)
Oh, you look really, really nice. Have you cut your hair?

SANDRA
Oh, fanks, yeah. Me daughter cut it with a pair of blunt scissors.

AMY (Confused)
Oh. Well it looks really good.

SANDRA
Yeah, me fuckin' neck is killing me... I'm in so much pain all the time... I fuckin' hate doctors, they don't know how to do their fuckin' job half the time... No one gives a shit and the government... well don't get me fuckin' started on them...

Silence from the group as everyone takes in Sandra's rant.

ADAM
So MOHAMMED, how was the programme? How did it go on Friday?

All of the group turn to face Mohammed, who is looking slightly concerned.

MOHAMMED
Oh yeah, well it was alright you know, but I kind of feel some sadness at the same time.

ADAM
Sadness? About what?

MOHAMMED
Well, you know when you leave primary school to go to secondary school?

Everybody nods with empathy; Sandra picks her feet.

MOHAMMED
Well, I feel a bit like that leaving this group and joining a new one. I really will miss everyone.

Amy smiles like a Cheshire cat at Mohammed to give him support.

ADAM

It's interesting why these feelings are coming up for you. Maybe it has something to do with your family dynamics... not feeling part of something... whereas here you do?

MOHAMMED

Yes, I think that's true, I felt like part of the group here. Like a family.

Silence from the group. Mohammed desperate for response and recognition.

SANDRA

Where's Dave? He's never here.

DAVID (Slightly irritated)

You mean Steve? Because Dave is here, I'm Dave. And it's David.

SANDRA

Oh yeah, sorry Dave—David. I always get you two mixed up.

DAVID (Frustrated)

I don't know why. Steve is never here.

SANDRA

Yeah, I know. That's why I mentioned it. One week he's here, the next he isn't. I can't fuckin' keep up.

DAVID
I've been trying very hard to get connected to him and when I do—the next week, he's not here. I find that really difficult.

SANDRA
I know. That's my point.

Judy is fidgeting in her chair; clearly the conversation is frustrating her.

ADAM
I think it's a fair point about Steve. We can ask him when he's back. What do others think in the group? Janine? Amy? What are your thoughts?

Janine shrugs and is hidden under her jacket.

AMY
I like Steve. I can understand the group's frustration... it obviously triggers emotions in people....

ADAM
What are those emotions for you?

AMY
Umm... not sure... big angry ones?

Judy has been showing signs of distress as Adam is yet to ask her opinion.

JUDY
What you're saying Sandra, is that it pisses you off when people miss sessions?

SANDRA
Well I do think that about Stee—

JUDY (Interrupts)
You don't know what his issues are; he's got stuff going on. You're pissed off at me for missing two sessions.

SANDRA (Slightly shocked)
No, I'm talking about Steve, not you.

JUDY
It's the same thing. You're two-faced.

ADAM
Okay, well this is interesting. What's going on for you, Judy? You seem really agitated with things.

JUDY
I just don't like people talking about others behind their back; they should be honest to their face.

DAVID
I did actually confront Steve last week.

SANDRA
I can't say it to his face, 'coz he's never here.

JUDY
People should just say it to my face that they're pissed off I missed those sessions.

DAVID
Judy, it's not that we're pissed off. We missed you—

JUDY
Nobody missed me. You were pissed off, just like you are with Steve.

Everyone speaks over each other (We did miss you... I missed you... etc.)

Silence from the group

MOHAMMED
You know, what I think Dave is trying to say is that—

DAVID (Interrupts)
Look I know I'm getting a bit touchy now, but I've never referred to myself as Dave. It's David.

SANDRA (To herself)
That is true. He kind of did say, 'it's Dave not David...'

MOHAMMED
Sorry, sorry, David. I think what David is trying to say is that we don't know have a connection with Steve.

ADAM
Were you going to say something, Amy?

Everyone waits to see if Amy contributes to the debate.

AMY (Pause)
Umm... No... I don't think so.

SANDRA
I mean the thing is, at the last meeting, I was in here putting plasters on me fuckin' feet yeah? 'Coz I couldn't walk with these fuckin' blisters, yeah? And he comes back in, Steve, yeah? And says 'What are you doing?' Yeah?

Sandra waits to see people's reaction. Clearly people don't understand her point.

SANDRA (CONT'D)
I mean, what sort of a bloke comes back to an empty room with a woman in there alone and says that?

Everyone stares blankly.

SANDRA (CONT'D) (About to cry)
I'm sorry but I just fuckin' hate men... Sorry no offence Dave—David.

Mohammed looks disheartened and everyone looks at him. Amy smiles. Long silence from the group.

DAVID
Well, I'm actually quite offended at that.

SANDRA
But I just said I didn't mean it towards you. I meant all men. Sorry, Mohammed.

                    DAVID
I don't feel like a man… I feel like a ten-year-old boy. You calling me a man, Sandra, doesn't make me a man… I need to feel like one…

                    ADAM
Maybe these feelings are connected with your father?

                    DAVID
Yes, I wanted to get close to my father. (Pause) I want to feel connected to a man…

He looks at Mohammed. Mohammed seems uncomfortable.

                    DAVID
Not in a… sexual way……just to connect. People just don't want to connect, and I find that really fucking hard. Steve not being here is again another man who I cannot connect with.

Judy's body language starts to indicate frustration.

                    JUDY (Outburst)
Like I said, Steve has stuff going on, just like I do. Has anyone bothered to ask me what's going on? No they haven't.

Long silence.

                    AMY (To Judy)
You've actually got a lot in common with David. He wants connection, and you want to be noticed.

Long silence whilst everyone takes in the comment from Amy. Amy gets up to grab a drink.

                ADAM (A little frustrated)
I think that's a really interesting point. What do you feel about what Amy has just said, Judy?

                        JUDY
I think she's probably right. My dad only noticed me when I did something wrong. He'd shout, throw things, hit me.

                       ADAM
What about when you did something right?

                        JUDY
He'd shout, throw things, hit me.

                        AMY
You must have felt like you didn't really exist.

                ADAM (Taking control)
I wondered if this feeling of being ignored resonates with anyone else in the group?

                      SANDRA
All the fuckin' time.

                      DAVID
Yes, well I—

David tries to speak, but then is ignored by Adam whilst he asks Janine.

ADAM
Janine, have you ever felt ignored?

JANINE
Yeah, but I like it. It means I don't have to talk.

MOHAMMED
Well, I've felt that everyone here listens and has made me feel so welcome

Steve enters.

MOHAMMED (CONT'D)
and allowed me to really be myself, you know. I just feel so sad to say goodbye to you all…

Steve enters very bold and brash, at a completely different pace to the group. He helps himself to tea whilst Mohammed tries to express his feelings. The group seems slighting agitated at Steve as they can't quite hear Mohammed.

STEVE
(Cuts in without noticing Mohammed was talking)
Sorry I'm late… I've just had the worst day already. I know I wasn't here last week, but there was a good reason for that. I've been given an ASBO from the local authority because they said I was getting up in some bird's face. But when someone steps in my front garden and asks me to clear my rubbish, what do they expect I'm gonna say?

David stands up and puts his hand out towards Steve.

DAVID
I'm pleased you're here, Steve.

Steve looks at the hand and doesn't go to shake it.

STEVE
Well... yeah, thanks, Dave mate. Cheers. I'm glad I got here, but it was touch and go for a while, you know.

David is rejected again by Steve and is clearly upset and sits down.

MOHAMMED
He doesn't like to be called 'Dave.'

DAVID (Angry)
Er, thank you, Mohammed. I can speak for myself; fight my own battles...

STEVE (Agitated)
Fight what, exactly?!

JUDY (Erupts)
Look Steve, I know you've got stuff going on, and you want to get it off your chest, but you've not been here for two sessions, and now you want to waltz in and take over. It's not on.

ADAM
Sorry Steve, but you have walked in, and we were kind of hearing from Mohammed, who is going to be leaving the group today to join the main programme.

STEVE
Oh sorry, I didn't know. Sorry, Mohammed.

SANDRA (Under her breath)
Well, if you'd been here...

STEVE (To Sandra)
What was that?

SANDRA
I said if you'd been here the last two weeks, you'd realise that Mohammed is leaving us.

STEVE (Angry)
What you accusing me of?

DAVID (Trying to be calm)
You see, Steve, we were all rather upset that you hadn't been here, and for me, I like to connect with people, and I felt that I haven't been able to do this with you because you haven't been here.

STEVE
Sorry, Dave, but I've got stuff going on, yeah?

MOHAMMED
Judy said that when you weren't here.

STEVE (Looking at Judy)
Oh, did she? And what the fuck would she know about what I've got going on?

ADAM (Calmly)
Really good to look at this stuff. I'm aware of the time, though, so Janine, did you bring your song?

Janine hides behind her coat and nods. The rest of the group are silent whilst the focus is on her. Steve and Judy are still fuming. David is close to tears.

ADAM
Well do you want to play it?

Janine shrugs.

MOHAMMED
I think it would be really good to hear your song, Janine.

Silence from the group. Janine gets up and puts her CD on. Michael Jackson's 'Man in the Mirror" plays out. The CD is scratched and plays through a Michael Jackson medley, jumping and skipping, until Amy turns it off.

ADAM
So JANINE, why that song today?

JANINE (Shrugs)
Just like it.

ADAM
Did you listen to it a lot when you were growing up?

Janine nods.

DAVID
I like Michael Jackson.

Various reactions from the group: nods, agreement noises,. Sandra is nodding off and not really engaging anymore.

ADAM
How long have you liked Michael Jackson?

JANINE
Since I was a baby.

ADAM
Were you very upset when he died?

JANINE (Close to tears)
Don't keep asking stuff.

ADAM
You must have felt a great loss when he died.

STEVE
I didn't.

The group look at Steve.

ADAM
Well everyone is different, Michael—

STEVE (Unimpressed)
Michael?

ADAM (To Janine)
—was probably there for you when others weren't—
like your father.

JANINE

Well, I know this sounds stupid, but if Michael and my dad were sat in a room, and a gun was held to their heads and you asked me which one I'd save, I'd save Michael.

Silence whilst people take in Janine's revelation as she buries herself under her coat.

STEVE

So, Judy... are you going to say it or am I?

Group seems confused and Sandra is back to picking her feet.

JUDY

Okay, well you brought it up, so you can say it...

STEVE

Me and Judy walked home the same way the other day...

DAVID

What's wrong with that?

STEVE

I've been taken for a mug, that's what! These boundaries are in place for a good reason: no socialising outside of the community. I get it now.

Judy is silent, but seething.

ADAM

How has it made you feel?

STEVE
Like a prize twat.

MOHAMMED
I think a walk is okay. I mean, it was just a walk...

STEVE
No, it wasn't. We ended up...

Group are all focused on Steve and what he is about to say.

STEVE
...we ended up going for a curry!

Silence. The group are clearly shocked, as there are clear rules about no socialising with other members of the group.

ADAM
Steve, you're obviously feeling very stirred up about this. It's good to look at why...

STEVE
Yeah, well I am. I didn't want to go for a curry... I felt I couldn't say no... I'm not ready for that...

AMY
How do you feel, Judy?

JUDY
Oh well, I'm glad that someone actually gives a shit about my feelings. There were two of us in the curry house. And Steve, I didn't hear you complaining at the time.

STEVE (Angry)
That's my point. I couldn't say no. I FELT LIKE I COULDN'T SAY NO!

ADAM
Okay, let's think about how we can work through this safely, for everyone. I think it's affecting others. Amy?

AMY
Oh, I'm fine. I'm used to violent situations after I was stabbed in the neck by my ex-boyfriend. I'm kind of numb to it now.

Silence from group.

ADAM
Okay, it's time. A minute's silence to reflect.

SANDRA
Yeah, so Steve, I need to say something—

Some members of the group shush her.

ADAM (Whispers)
It's a minute silence, Sandra.

SANDRA (Whispers)
Who said?

ADAM
I did…

Sandra gestures to her lips and mouths 'sorry.' Steve is clearly fuming as he's about to be attacked again.

ADAM
Okay, well that's it. But before we go, is there anything else you want to say, Mohammed, before you leave us?

MOHAMMED
Well, I'm just really going to miss you all, and thanks for everything. I know this is a bit much, but I just really feel like I want to give people a hug.

Janine darts out first. Judy is staring at a wall as if she is going to put her fist through it. Steve gets up and walks off. Sandra begins putting another plaster on her feet.

SANDRA
Absolutely not. Sorry, Mohammed, but you know my thoughts on that.

Everyone else leaves before they have to answer or hug, apart from David, who is hovering.

DAVID
Oh, Mohammed, I'll give you a hug!

David throws his arms around him, tight and awkward, whilst everyone leaves and Adam is left clearing the chairs.

~END~

Little Episodes
Mission Statement

These days, the artistic and entertainment industries can generate seriously big money. While this may be palatable enough for the lucky few that get picked to 'succeed', it is alienating and depressing for the hoards of equally talented creatives lost in a sea of penniless artists. Huge marketing bodies dictate who is to be the next 'talent to watch' and who is now dispensable, with the onus always on super-stardom rather than working artists. Although not every consumer lets the powers that be sway their taste and personal choice, the artistic industries are tightly controlled and many interesting, original and talented artists simple get starved out of the running.

I was a 'resting' actress, simultaneously penning a novel and teaching part-time at an inner London college when I met Chris Colston—he was eeking a living from a small painting commission. We sat, one summer's day on a sweaty Southbank, and ranted about the restraints and pure luck needed to earn any kind of crust from an artistic career. We felt guilty that we couldn't bend our minds to become decent accountants or train drivers and berated ourselves for our inability to be happy enough in an office job of some description.

After a second round of tap waters, we decided the only option was to expand upon the 'Expression of Depression' anthologies we were already printing—books featuring work from unknowns alongside successful writers—and branch out to encompass other artistic mediums. We had a vision of collaborating with talented individuals to bypass the lottery of the big industries and take high quality art straight to an audience bored of being dictated to.

Little Episodes is an independent publisher and arts production company run by pro-active artists. We curate art exhibitions, put on poetry nights, gigs and plays, publish books, run an online social network and forum and are soon to open a café/bar.

- Our belief is that the world is a better place with artistic expression.
- Art can be a powerful tool to incite empathy and understanding.
- We provide ourselves and others with an artistic platform.
- We provide an audience with an alternative to mainstream entertainment.

LUCIE BARÂT 2011